MANAGING YOURSELF

The Mike Pedler Library
Developing people and organizations
General Editor: Dr Mike Pedler
Published by Lemos & Crane, London

Also available in this series:

John Burgoyne
**Developing Yourself, Your Career
and Your Organization**

Nancy M. Dixon
Dialogue at Work

Rennie Fritchie and Malcolm Leary
Resolving Conflicts in Organizations

Mike Pedler and Kath Aspinwall
A Concise Guide to the Learning Organization

Reg Revans
ABC of Action Learning

*"The books are easy to read, well set out and full of useful prompts and
activities that will aid managers in explaining key issues.".*
Chris Bones, HR Director Europe, UDV

For more information visit us at **www.lemosandcrane.co.uk**

Managing Yourself

MIKE PEDLER AND
TOM BOYDELL

Lemos&**Crane**

This edition first published in Great Britain 1999

Lemos & Crane
20 Pond Square
Highgate Village
London N6 6BA
http://www.lemosandcrane.co.uk

ISBN 1-898001-55-3

A CIP catalogue record for this book is available from the British Library.

Designed and typeset by DAP Ltd, London.
Printed and bound by Redwood Books, Trowbridge.

Contents

Introduction to the Library

"All learning is for the sake of action, and all action for the sake of friendship." John Macmurray

The supposed end of certainty, and with it the arts of prediction and strategic planning, has led some managers to contemplate notions of paradox, chaos and boundlessness, multiple dilemmas and complexity theory. Others, struggling with the intractable problems of organization, have turned to re-engineering and quality management, only to find that these apparently novel solutions turn out to be old wine in new bottles, the descendants of Taylorism and Fordism.

To be responsive to change, a child, adult, organization, even a society, must be adept at learning. Learning is the means of acquiring new knowledge and skill, but also of making sense of our lives – individually and collectively – in increasingly fragmented times. In the absence of a reliable plan or blueprint for success, we can go on hopefully to learn our way forwards, recognizing what we cannot do, yet growing in confidence, making our own path.

For individuals, a fourth 'R' – Responsive to Change – must now be added to the traditional school curriculum of Reading, Writing and Arithmetic. The individual learner is at the heart of organizations and societies grappling with unprecedented change and its consequences. Only those able to create some measure of order in themselves can create order and purpose in those around them. In the absence of predictable employment, careers and lives, we must become adept at learning new ways, new identities.

For organizations, with an average lifespan of forty years and declining, learning has become essential for survival (De Geus). Organizational learning as also been suggested as the only sustainable source of competitive advantage (Senge) and the single most important quality that can be developed and traded (Garratt).

In communities and society new efforts at partnership, collaborative action and learning in public forums to tackle the 'wicked' problems of poverty, inequality, pollution, crime and public safety are replacing the old choices of left or right, public or private, electoral democracy or entrepreneurial leadership.

When we discard old mind-sets, search for new directions, learning is at a premium. At all levels the questions are the same: how can we develop what we do best in order to trade and learn *and* avoid the undesirable downsides? How can we release individual energy, potential, self-reliance, active citizenship *and* build wealth, well-being, collective security and the quality of all our lives?

★

If individuals who are able to manage and develop themselves are the cornerstones of this new society, it is equally plain that in an era characterized by large organizations, that learning must extend to wider relationships in teams, companies, and increasingly, between organizations themselves. The new optimism of the 'learning organization' has emerged as part of this understanding, but even this does not go far enough. There are problems aplenty to defeat even the very best of our organizations standing alone; there is a need to organize action and learning in coalitions and partnerships of agencies to respond to these pressing tasks.

The need is scarcely yet glimpsed, let alone grasped, but in an ideal collaboration such as a 'learning society', there is: a freedom to learn – and not to learn – for individuals; an organizational desire to support the learning of all members and stakeholders *and* a vision to transform the organization as a whole in creating new products, services and relationships; together with equal opportunities in learning for all citizens, not least so that they might contribute to communities and societies that are good places in which to live. This manifesto is of course a re-interpretation of old revolutionary aspirations: *Liberty* for individuals, the ruling value of *Fraternity* for organizations, and a duty of *Equality* of treatment and opportunity in the social sphere. To each of these we hope to make a contribution, with ideas ranging from personal self-development, through organizational learning to transformations in communities and social policies.

★

The books in the Library are concerned with learning and action on the pressing issues facing us as people living and working in organizations, cities and societies. And whilst there is no single philosophy here, there is an implied criticism of the economic and cultural consensus which underlies much of the business and management literature in particular. There are challenges here for those who tend to assume that our future rests on the 'roll out' of global, information-based capitalism supported by the spread of liberal democracy. There is support for those who question whether the individual and organizational development aimed at 'high performance' or 'excellence' always leads to desirable outcomes. The irony of the self-proclaimed 'learning organization' which is still not a healthy place for people to work in or to live next to, is also noted.

Action and learning require more than just good ideas. In terms of content, each book in the Library contains:

- *educational input:* ideas of substance that you need to know about

- *invitations to action:* suggestions in the texts when you stop reading and go to do something with the ideas in order to learn

- *ethical and political elements:* moral support in action and learning about being an honest colleague, seeking good purposes or doing the right thing in difficult circumstances for those operating in dilemma-laden territory.

Though they aim to be attractive and accessible these books are not 'easy reads'. They offer the reader an invitation to self-confrontation. Suspicious of easy answers and not content with theory, they offer a middle ground of active methods and approaches to the problems and questions posed. Even on questions to which there are no obvious solutions, there are directions to follow to engage your personal energies, the support of colleagues and the aspirations of clients and customers. I hope you can't put one of these books down without at least thinking of doing something differently.

MIKE PEDLER

Introduction

This book is for managers and for people who want to become managers; people who combine *both* doing *and* thinking. A central idea is that you cannot manage others unless you are able to manage yourself - being proactive, rather than being buffeted and controlled by other people and external events. This means working from the inside out; from managing yourself to managing the world around you.

We live in what has been called a transitional age - an era in which old ways of doing things are continually being replaced by new ways. Nowhere is this more true than in managing. This book is intended for people who are only too aware that times are changing, and who are conscious of the importance of:

- releasing people and organizations from old patterns of thought and action and unleashing the pent-up creative energies within that at present go unrecognized, unrewarded, unwanted

- empowering individuals so that they can shake off their dependency on increasingly inexpert experts, and instead develop their own expertise

- considering the whole person; managing ideas, feelings, and actions; working with the physical, mental and spiritual parts of ourselves

- the acceleration of scientific and technological change and also of growth of information, which is even faster

- the fundamental relationships between 'work'/'home',

'work'/'leisure', 'employment'/'unemployment', which are being challenged and reassessed

- the imbalances in the world with regard to the distribution of food, power and freedom and all the other aspects of human society, and yet ...

- ... the growing sense that we are 'one world'; part of a connected whole so that other people, or other parts of the organization, or other parts of the world, cannot just be ignored or seen as enemies to be defeated

- that although the idea of managing is straightforward enough, it is often very difficult and complex to put into practice; and that simplistic solutions to problems, although appearing attractive, are actually illusory.

To manage effectively in this world, action must be taken in full awareness of what the consequences might be for me, for others, for my organization and for the environment.

★

In the fifteen years since we first wrote this book, the case for managing yourself has grown stronger. The moral case was established long ago when emerging modern man was urged to 'know thyself' by the inscription on the Temple of Apollo. Since then, making the best of ourselves, for ourselves, for others and for the force of good in the world has been a core tenet of humanism. This personal quest remains as vital as ever, but alongside the philosophical injunction, there are pressing contemporary reasons for knowing and managing yourself.

Few of today's organizations offer jobs for life. It would be foolish to rely on an organization to plan your career or to provide the training and learning required for your survival, maintenance and development. Opportunities certainly exist but it is your responsibility to make the best of them. Where once institutions provided and decided - your progression, pension plan, retirement options and so on - these are now your responsibilities.

Where do you start? Ensuring employability and, most importantly, making the most of yourself and of your potential, rests upon being able to manage yourself. You need to be fit, whole, balanced, ready and able to tackle new challenges and opportunities.

The essence of managing yourself - integrating thought and action to realize change, development and relationships with others - resonates with the spirit or *zeitgeist* of this transitional age. The consequences of the individualistic thinking of the 1980s have now become clear. The extremes of that thinking - 'there's no such thing as society, only individuals and families' and even 'greed is good' - are reflected in the widening disparities between rich and poor, in the gross divisions in cities and communities, in increasing personal tensions and social exclusion. There is now much talk of 'joined-up thinking' to address the 'wicked problems' of crime, health inequality and poverty. There is a shift towards integration and inclusion: development through participation and the involvement of all of those who share the problem to create healthier communities and livelier organizations. The stand-alone provision of health, welfare, education, social and other services is blurring into multi-agency working. Joint planning has become essential. For individuals the balance is swinging away from an emphasis on personal survival, not back to an earlier philosophy of cradle-to-grave welfare provision, but towards a third way, in which rights come balanced with responsibilities to others.

In work organizations, the drive to create learning companies is fuelled by a climate of accelerating change and global competition. The learning organization seeks to integrate inner and outer through sustainable development with the environment in which it markets its services and finds its resources. In turn learning organizations provide a good environment for people able to manage themselves to achieve their full potential in working collaboration with other individuals. Indeed such organizations depend heavily on people who can create personal energy and direction and spread this outwards to colleagues, work groups and business partners.

Change in the big picture can start with change in yourself. *Managing Yourself* offers a vision which balances individualism and environmentalism in an expression of 'both...and....' rather than 'either...or...' thinking. Integrating the inner and outer opens up many possibilities within and for friends and colleagues in families, groups, organizations and even in society as a whole. The potential rewards are great but picking up this challenge takes enthusiasm and commitment as well as support from others.

★

In keeping with our belief in combining thought and action, we have written this book in a way that activates and brings it to life by recruiting you - the reader - to go through a process of exploring various aspects of managing yourself. This involves:

- warming up to the subject; developing an interest in it

- shedding light on it; analysing, looking in depth

- weighing things up; deciding what it means for you in terms of action

- grounding, or carrying out the action, and then reviewing what you have done.

This is done in a variety of ways including 'warming-up' questionnaires and case studies, together with activities, exercises and reflections for you to improve and develop the way you manage yourself. However there is no one-size-fits-all solution here - your interests and experiences form the cornerstone in this book and indeed will determine how you go about reading and acting on it.

There are 17 Activities here to encourage you into action and they are designed to help you reflect on your experiences. For ease of reference these are collected together in a workbook (following Chapter 8) and they will engage you in an active consideration of some of the new perspectives on managing and self-managing. This is a self-empowering process and one of the powers you will develop in this process is that of finding your own knowledge - rather than relying on others to provide it for you.

In addition, and throughout the book, there are 16 practical exercises. Unlike the workbook Activities, some of these need to be done on a regular weekly or daily basis. After all, you can't expect to get physically fit simply by going for one two-mile run, and some of these exercises won't produce any benefits at all unless they are carried out regularly. You need gradually to build up a regime of exercise, appropriate to you, your needs, your starting level and your goals. For example, it may suit you to work through all the activities and exercises as you work through the book. For other people it will be preferable to concentrate, in the first instance, on a few activities and exercises that seem right for them. You can always come back to the others later.

Because the book is written to involve you, it may in parts surprise you, challenging, as it does, some taken-for-granted ideas about management that we think are no longer good enough. So, approach this book with an open mind, but don't believe everything we say: work with it, reflect on it and come to your own conclusions.

We look at the question of managing oneself in more depth in Chapter 1, working with various models of self-management. Then, in Chapters 2 to 6, these aspects are explored in more detail, starting with the planning and carrying out of *action* in Chapter 2. Chapters 3 and 4 then look at *knowing, valuing* and *being* yourself, followed by managing yourself and your *skills* (Chapter 5) and your *health* (Chapter 6). We then move further outwards from the self. It is clear that in order to learn to manage ourselves properly, we need other people to challenge and support us. Chapter 7 looks at this in some detail. Similarly, because you manage yourself within some organizational context, Chapter 8 is devoted to organizational considerations.

1 First Manage Yourself

The fundamental assumption behind this book is that anyone who wants to improve the way they manage others must first learn to manage him or herself. The argument is that if a person can create order and purpose in their lives then they have taken the first step to creating order and purpose amongst others and in the wider working environment. This fundamental assumption can be disputed. Surely, you might say, even some of our greatest managers and leaders have appeared calm and in control whilst battling internal turmoil and chaos? Everyone has some experience of putting personal troubles to one side, whilst soldiering on in a job or role which is important to others. Later in this chapter, we discuss the notion of the person as being always in a process of becoming something different and being, at any one time, either developing, maintaining or surviving. In this last survival mode it is often necessary to split ourselves temporarily, the outside appearance being very different from the inner reality. However, if this splitting continues over a long time it does not aid development and can even be harmful to us and others, possibly leading to illness.

So, our dictum is, for the healthy development of self and others: first manage yourself. Learn to manage from the inside out, starting with managing me and then moving out to managing the people and the world around you.

To start, think about the way you are currently managing yourself. Consider the link between what went well or badly by turning now to Activity 1 on p.170.

ACTIVITY 1 Page 170

Managing from inside to out rests on the idea that what is outside is a reflection of what is inside. This suggests that the way a person acts as a manager is likely to be based upon the way they manage themselves and their immediate environment. I cannot really manage things outside of me until I can manage my inner self. Conversely, I cannot really manage myself until I can manage my outer world. This is shown in Figure 1.1.

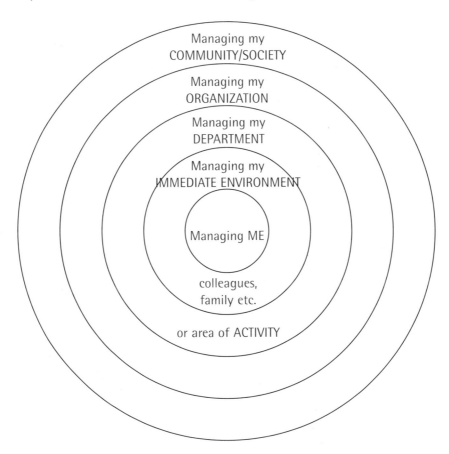

Fig 1.1 Managing from the inside out

With these levels or categories in mind, now try a simple personal audit set out in Activity 2 on p.172.

For most of us, there are some aspects of our lives that we are managing well at any one time, and others that we are managing badly. If you could not think of any in the 'doing well' category, this is probably because you are making a poor job of managing your self-image; you are failing - or refusing - to recognize and value your talents. Chapter 4 looks at this in some detail. Conversely, if everything seems perfect, then either you have no need for this book, or you are a bit short on self-knowledge - see Chapter 3.

You are your own best case study; that's why we suggested working on Activity 2. However, other people's situations can form the basis for comparison. Here is an extract from a day in the life of Peter Ford, a human resources executive with a bank. At thirty-nine, Peter has climbed the promotion ladder quickly and some colleagues envy him his success, his energy and obvious commitment; he is earmarked as a future director - although no one has told him so. Now read on:

CASE STUDY

Peter Ford arrives at his office at 7.30am, fifteen minutes earlier than usual but fifteen minutes later than he had planned. He'd come in early to clear his desk, but after a heavy social evening the night before, he was scarcely warmed up by his tea and toast and the largely automatic exchanges with members of the family about at that hour. The traffic had been just as bad as it was at his normal time - and all those e-mails waiting for him before the main events of the day! Peter dashes up to his floor, nods 'hello' to the Head of Foreign in the foyer, but fails to notice the greeting of the receptionist, all the time hoping that he won't meet any colleague who might hold him up.

1.30 p.m.: lunch. In the half an hour available before meeting his HR colleagues to discuss a contentious incentive scheme to promote manager mobility, Peter eats a sandwich and sips coffee while working through some remaining e-mails. After long practice he can hold the telephone between his left shoulder and cheek while writing answers to memos, letters and so on. That's one of the reasons he has been successful. Compared with some of his colleagues he seems able to cram twelve hours of work into a ten-hour day. The morning had disappeared under the assault of three meetings. The 9.00 a.m. one to agree some new role descriptions had dragged on for two hours thanks to Ken Wallington's tedious nit-picking. During this time Peter noticed he had a headache, although the next meeting with Pam Walton and John Novarra had been more fun and he had been sorry when he'd had to rush off to attend the boss's weekly briefing.

He stopped writing for a moment, put down the phone and massaged the left side of his neck: rheumatism, no doubt! He thought about the rest of the day: more meetings, at least two hours of dictating, reading and corrections, and then off for the Edinburgh shuttle and tonight's dinner before tomorrow's conference. Not much time for relaxation there, and certainly more food and drink than was good for him. And next week in Paris will be worse - the price of success!

Momentarily he felt sorry for himself. Why did he always take on too much? Why hadn't he said 'No' to that conference? He knew the answer to this one - his own need to keep tabs on everything, to know what was going on, to keep himself in the limelight.

So much of his life was like this now. Not only was the job more demanding and complex, but he seemed to have to spend more and more time politicking to stay up with the field. Actually, when he thought about it, Peter didn't like that part of himself very much. He could fight and struggle for power and resources along with the rest, but did he want to live like this? He could do without the snide comments and aggression, the calculation and the secrecy.

On the rare occasions when he stopped to think about it, he had a nagging feeling that a lot of what he did was not all that important anyway, it was all self-generated. What was it achieving - for himself or for anyone else? In what way could the world be said to be a better place because of him? Sometimes the thought of spending another twenty-five years doing this was . . . well, it sent a shudder through him.

Other people didn't put in the hours he did. . . . And then the human contact was not all it could be. You were always pushing, chasing people for work and so on. Surely you should have time to relax, to make jokes, to have fun . . . ? And, he concluded, the kids were growing up fast and without a lot of help from him. Since Sam had returned to work and become interested in her own career, the times when they coincided in giving their full attention to each other were few and far between. . . .

2.00p.m.: Peter dumps his cup and sandwich wrapper in the bin, puts on his jacket, picks up his pen, diary and note pad, and heads for room 202. . . .

· ·

The picture is clear; though in many ways a successful manager, Peter Ford's life is a mess. He is on a treadmill powered partly by his own inner compulsions and partly by the demands of colleagues, boss, customers, clients . . . even making time for friends and family feels like another pressure. If he doesn't stop himself soon, something else probably will. Yet how can he break out of this state, this man-made mould, this patiently accumulated self-image?

How much of Peter do you see in yourself? It's easier to see from the outside; to notice the mistakes and traps that others fall into (although Peter's colleagues had quite a different view of him from that revealed by these inner thoughts - and what did his wife and family think?).

How well can you see yourself? How good a job are you doing at managing both yourself and the world around you?

This process can be seen as a continuous and connected flow; flowing out from you into contact with others, giving to them and receiving from them, hence flowing back into yourself, changing, learning and developing inwards as well as outwards. We can superimpose this 'double-loop' of learning on Figure 1.1 to show this continuous, dynamic flow of movement, from inner to outer and outer back to inner, and so on, shown now in Figure 1.2, below.

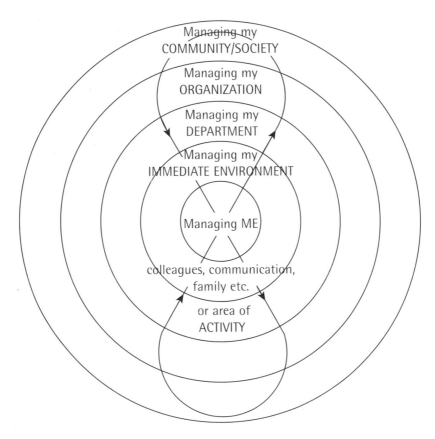

Fig 1.2: Managing from the inside out

FROM 'EITHER ... OR...' TO 'BOTH ... AND ...' THINKING

This idea can be taken a step further. We have stressed that the inner and outer worlds are inextricably linked. If you take the loop out from Figure 1.2 and redraw it on its own, then which part of this loop is the most important? Clearly, it is impossible to say for the loop cannot exist without both parts, just as you can't have a one-sided coin. This apparently simple notion has great significance; it is an example of changing from 'either ... or ...' (either the inner or the outer is the most important) to 'both ... and ...' thinking (both the inner and the outer are important). Joined-up thinking - thinking in a way that brings things together, rather than polarizes them - is the key to many of today's problems and dilemmas, personal and organizational.

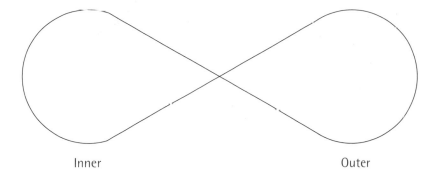

Inner   Outer

Fig 1.3 : Inner/Outer

Take for example the question of management development. This has often concentrated on an outer world of models and theories of economics, business, markets, and so on. Even when learning about people, the emphasis has focussed on *other* people - what motivates them, what makes them tick. Moreover, the *process* as well as the content of management education tends to be outer-oriented, assuming that we learn best from a diet of pre-digested knowledge and distilled wisdom from the past.

This is a conservative tradition that actually hinders learning how to manage, amounting to what Reg Revans has called 'the idolization of past experience'. By concentrating its content on the outer world, and by using methods that do not encourage the flow of learning back and forth between the inner and the outer, much management education imposes severe limitations on creativity and learning.

Such education places great faith in, and emotional dependency on, 'experts', which works against the necessity of thinking for oneself. Experts provide scarce and valued knowledge or skills but this does not protect them from being used to support questionable causes. In fact their specialist but narrow knowledge tends to make them more vulnerable to abuse in serving the ends of commercial or political masters. Have you noticed how the 'independent experts' appointed by this business, or that industry, come up with very different opinions from those retained by competitors or by protest movements? Paulo Freire said that education is either for liberation or for domination; reliance on expert opinion leads to domination, managing yourself leads towards liberation.

For better or for worse, the day of unquestioned expertise is gone. Instead we need, in this era of rapid and unpredictable change, to develop the confidence and ability to act and to learn from action. Whilst we may seek information or advice from others, the aim is to think for ourselves and to come to our own decisions. This is not to belittle the wisdom of the past, but to hold it in its proper perspective. We are not elevating navel-gazing over book learning or calling for action at the expense of understanding. We do want to strengthen a new tradition of self-development.

What are its main features? As noted in this chapter, this approach to self-development takes a 'both ... and ...' view of managing and developing; thus, it focuses:

- both on the inner and the outer, recognizing that in general these are inextricably linked, and that neither can really be understood in isolation from the other

- on managing both myself and my environment - again in the realization that I cannot understand or manage others until I can understand or manage myself *and that conversely* ... I cannot understand or manage myself until I can understand and manage others

- on being responsible to and for both myself and my environment - that is, I need to understand and take into account both my own needs and those of others *and*... I need to understand and be aware of the consequences of my actions both for myself and for others

- both on theory and on practice - by using my real-life questions, issues and problems as the basic starting point in my need and search for established knowledge *and by*... using my real-life experiences as an opportunity to derive and generate my own meanings and understandings.

So how can we make a start on this? What is inside that inner circle in Figure 1.1 (Managing me)?

Survival, development and maintenance

As noted at the outset of this chapter, at any given time at home, work or elsewhere, a person can be described as engaged in survival, development or maintenance. Surviving means keeping going when things seem pretty awful; not going under, keeping your head above water, avoiding collapse, disaster or destruction. Although it can be seen as a minimal level of functioning, rather than a desirable one, it is something that we all experience, and that each of us, at times, recognizes as the best we can do, the most we can hope for.

At this point it would be useful to examine some of your own survival experiences. Working with Activity 3 on p.174 enables you to do this.

One of the things that may have emerged from working on Activity 3 is the importance of support while struggling to survive. Some seek the support of tranquilizers, which may be essential in the short-term but don't really have anything positive to offer in the long run. (This is also true of other forms of instant support, such as alcohol.) Far better - although perhaps harder to come by - is the support of other people, either individually or in a group (on this, see especially Chapter 7). Not only can this support keep you going when you just might give up, but also it can help you gradually to make sense out of what is happening, so that you can begin moving again. W. Edwards Deming once remarked ironically of companies that 'survival is not compulsory' - but every crisis survived can make us stronger when we move into development mode.

DEVELOPMENT

As you did in Activity 3, think now about three or four occasions in your life when you feel you have developed. What were these occasions? How did you feel at the time? What were the effects on you, and on others around you?

Some of these developmental events may be the same survival episodes that you have already considered. Although not all crises lead to development, nor is all development brought about by crisis, there is often a link between the two; why should this be? Although the term is often used loosely, in this book development refers to a qualitative change in the way you are. Development can mean:

- bringing out what is latent or potential

- bringing to a more advanced state

- working out potentialities

- causing to grow or advance

- advancing through successive stages to a more fully grown state

- opening out.

What does this mean for a person's development as a manager? It might mean a new skill, a new way of seeing things, a fresh attitude, an unfamiliar set of feelings, a new level of consciousness, or a different mode of managing (see Chapter 3). The important word in all of these is *new:* development is not just more of the same, more knowledge, or a higher degree of an existing skill. Development involves a different quality of being or functioning, rather than a mere topping up of something that you already have.

Gregory Bateson said that all learning arises from difference and this is why the starting point for development is often experienced as a 'crisis' or perturbation. It is when we get a surprise or a shock, when things deviate from the expected or start to go wrong, that we come face to face with the realization that our existing views on the world, on work, on relationships, etc. are no longer as valid as we thought previously. Here is another short case example:

CASE STUDY

Musa Mohammed had carefully climbed the promotion ladder in an engineering company, and is now, at 42, an assistant chief design engineer with confident expectations of succeeding his retiring boss. It comes as a severe shock to be told that it had been decided to appoint from outside, in order to bring new ideas into the company.

Musa's view - of the company, his job, himself - has suddenly been invalidated. How can he respond to this? Obviously, one way is to become bitter and angry. Indeed, disbelief followed by anger is the usual reaction to severe shock or crisis; the important thing is to be aware of this, survive it and eventually to move on, rather than retaining the experience inside as negativity.

This is where support is so vital. Musa is lucky in this respect. He has a good friend who is not only supportive in the traditional sense, but who also cares enough for him to take the risk of giving Musa some feedback. So after several weeks of listening sympathetically, he suggests that his friend perhaps has been a bit of a 'stick-in-the-mud', that he has in fact at times refused to consider or dismissed new ideas.

At first Musa can't believe his ears. Here is his old friend more or less saying, 'It's all your own fault.' However, deep down inside he is able to recognize that there is some truth here. Gradually, very slowly at first, and again with support from friends, family and his new boss, he changes his image of himself, realizing that he has to develop a new attitude towards innovation. He then goes on to start finding out much more about latest thinking, which he is surprised to find very stimulating to his own ideas. After three years his whole approach to the job has changed, and he much more looks the part for a more senior post, either within his present company or elsewhere.

· ·

Musa's crisis turns out to be the first, precipitating step towards development. Initial feelings of disbelief, anger, dismay, pain, grief, among others, can be transformed into the starting point for development, especially if we have a network of support to keep us going. The alternative, leading to a more or less permanent slide into continuing anger, depression, de-motivation or even self-destruction, is all too easy. This is covered in greater depth in Chapter 3.

Another link between shock and development arises from the fact that, in acquiring a new perspective on the world, we are letting go of part of our former selves. This is very likely to be stressful, since we are in effect saying goodbye to something that has been important to us. Even when we can clearly see that the change is for the better, it is often hard to let go of a cherished idea, value, ambition, relationship, person, job, place or whatever. Often, at this stage, we are beset with doubt, or guilt, or a feeling of not having made the best use of time or opportunities in the past.

When Tom's eldest daughter Alison left home at the age of eighteen, she went on good terms with no feelings of rancour or rejection. The whole thing was a very natural development – Alison became independent and Tom became the father of an independent woman, as opposed to a dependent girl. Nonetheless, for some time after he was filled with feelings of regret and doubts as to whether he could have been 'a better father', mooning over family photographs and so on. Even developments that come our way naturally, and are basically 'good' from the start, are often experienced as shocks or crises.

MAINTENANCE

So where does maintenance come in? An obvious example is that of physical maintenance or keeping fit. People cope better with either survival or development if they are physically fit. But what about more general fitness? Indeed, what does the word 'fit' mean? Chambers Dictionary gives as its main definition 'in suitable condition' and 'well trained and ready'. Maintenance can be seen as getting ready for development - keeping up to date, watching what's going on, keeping in good physical condition, building and maintaining a support network, and acquiring certain skills (such as observation, reflection, self-awareness) that are needed to transform crisis into development. Maintenance is also vital in recuperating from surviving.

More than surviving, but less than developing, perhaps we may sometimes settle for maintenance and avoid the challenges of change and development. The question for the keep-fit freak is 'What am I getting ready for?' Figure 1.4. shows maintenance between surviving and developing with arrows illustrating the linkage of all three in a continuous flow. Again, this is a case of 'both ... and...' rather than 'either ... or ...'. Getting ready, keeping fit, is very useful provided you realize you are getting ready to do something; developing is fine, but if you don't spare time for maintenance or consolidation you will wear yourself out with frenzied changes.

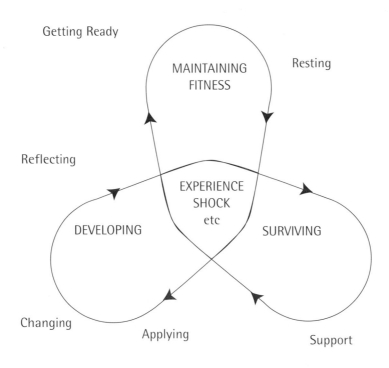

Figure 1.4: Skills Maintenance and Development

HEALTH, SKILLS, ACTION AND IDENTITY

If surviving, maintaining and developing describe the process involved in managing me, then what is the output or product of these efforts? Broadly speaking, there are four aspects of ourselves that we need to help survive, maintain and develop:

- health: a sound mind in a sound body

- skills: mental, technical, social, artistic

- action: getting things done in the world

- identity: knowing who you are, accepting yourself while having an idea of who you want to become.

Though separated here, these four form a whole: your health helps you to get things done; action is helped by skill, and by the motivation which comes from the way you see and value yourself. Figure 1.5 shows this relationship:

Skills

Action in
the world

Health   Identity

Figure 1.5: Health, Skills, Action and Identity

Action is focal since, in the end, as a manager it is what you do that matters. Good health, skills and self-identity lose much of their point without application to some useful end. We can illustrate the interplay of these factors from the experience of another manager:

CASE STUDY

Marion Anderson applied a few months ago for secondment to an exciting new project. Unfortunately, she was interviewed by an extremely aggressive senior manager, who challenged her ability to tackle the assignment and made sexist remarks from the outset.

Marion became flustered, and the interview went badly. As a result she labelled herself as 'no good at interviews' - i.e. part of her self-image is that of someone who is, and therefore always will be, unable to handle an interview properly.

Now her boss has put her forward to be reconsidered. She has many of the qualifications and qualities required for the project, but she still has her negative self-image as far as interviews are concerned. Consequently, she feels uncertain and wants to do well but when the time comes she doesn't have the confidence and will to overcome this and becomes tongue-tied; she isn't able to do herself justice or to show her true capabilities.

....

Looking back on Marion's experience, especially in the second interview, reveals the interplay of:

- labelling herself as 'no good at interviews', i.e. thinking of herself as a bad interviewee

- feeling uncertain and unconfident and,

- lacking the willpower to overcome this, to do herself justice.

Here is an all too familiar vicious circle where lack of skill (in handling unfair confrontation or criticism) leads to a negative view of the self, which in turn reduces skill even further. Marion's negative thoughts and unconfident feelings reinforce each other so that her intention or desire to do well is overpowered. Consequently, she is unable to manage herself in the way she would have liked. These three basic inner processes influence our actions all the time. Managing yourself involves managing your:

- thinking: your ideas, thoughts, perceptions, theories, beliefs, values

- feeling: your emotions, moods, feelings

- willing or doing: your intentions, motives, drives.

As shown in the examples of both Musa and Marion, working on your sense of identity, your self-image, is vital in managing me. Below, we have put together the four aspects of the self that need managing - action, identity, skills, and health, - with the three inner processes of thinking, feeling and willing. This table on p.24 sums up the characteristics or attributes required in successfully managing yourself and indeed other people. It also illustrates the format of this book, showing which chapters deal with which attributes.

MANAGING ME IS OK!

Before moving on, however, what about all the others with whom we work and live? Perhaps the case is made for managing me as far as you the reader are concerned; if you could manage your goals and priorities and survive, maintain and develop the thinking, feeling and willing aspects of your health, skills, action and identity, then clearly you'll be making progress.

The most obvious criticism of the managing me argument is that it is selfish. A self-managing approach involves thinking about and looking after yourself; it starts from *your* needs, strengths, weaknesses, goals, and so on. But if managing is first and foremost about working with and through other people, then surely focusing on oneself in this way is self-indulgent, even narcissistic?

We come up here against two opposing traditions in managing - one of selfless denial, the other of selfish domination. One tradition holds that managers should do the job in a selfless way, seeing themselves not only in charge of, but also responsible for, other people. There is much that is valuable in this view; few think highly of the captain who is first into the lifeboats. Nonetheless, if this belief means that you do not think about yourself enough to keep up to date, or learn new skills, or look after yourself and spend time with your family, then as a manager you are not only failing

TABLE 1: ASPECTS OF THE SELF THAT REQUIRE MANAGING

Inner processes that require managing

	Thinking	*Feeling*	*Willing or doing*	
Action in the world: getting things done	Ability to make your own decisions, for yourself, as well as being open to suggestions and feed back from others. Decisions made with an understanding of the way in which your actions affect other people, and have consequences for them as well as for you.	Concern both for your own interests and for those of other people - thus, making moral decisions.	Going out and taking initiatives; courage. Managing and transforming setbacks, disappointments, frustration; determination.	See Chapter 2
Identity, self	Personal values, ethical and moral standards, and philosophical, spiritual and/or religious beliefs. Awareness and understanding of these and of other aspects of self. Knowing yourself.	Recognizing your strengths and rejoicing in them; accepting yourself in spite of your weaknesses. Valuing yourself.	Self-motivation, purpose in life; sense of security, faith and hope. Being yourself.	See Chapters 3 and 4
Skills	Mental and conceptual skills; e.g., memory, logic, creativity, intuition.	Interpersonal, social, expressive and artistic skills.	Physical, mechanical and technical skills.	See Chapter 5
Health: a sound mind in a sound body	Holistic thinking, which includes avoidance of simplistic stereotyping and compartmentalizing: recognition of the way in which things are interrelated and interdependent: thinking in terms of 'both . . . and . . .'. Ability to remain open-minded, to suspend judgement.	Awareness and acknowledgement of feelings (you have feelings, rather than feelings having you). Balance, inner calm.	Physical exercise, diet, nutrition. Healthy habits and lifestyle.	See Chapter 6

yourself but also setting a bad example for others.

A managing me first approach might often seem to fall into the other tradition - that of self-interestedness, whatever the cost to others. Thus, it might seem selfish to people used to seeing you behave more selflessly; perhaps more importantly, it may seem selfish and 'wrong' to you yourself, because you are saying, in effect, 'Now it's my turn.' To say, for example, 'From now on I'm going to take half a day a week out to read and to think', or to say, 'You and the children can look after yourselves a bit more because I'm going out to work' requires courage. It also requires skill to get the balance right.

Our early upbringing provides many useful ideas and rules about behaving responsibly and thinking of others. Most children eventually learn to share their toys and take their turn, and by late adolescence most of us learn not just to think of ourselves, but to recognize that others have rights too. Later, as mothers, fathers, husbands, wives, managers, neighbours, we get a lot of practice at putting the needs of others first, and it is possible to get out of balance - neglecting our own needs, or thinking that these needs, although felt, are not really legitimate.

One problem with always behaving selflessly is that you can become stuck - with being taken for granted, stuck with all the jobs no one else wants, as well as being stuck with yourself because you can't change, move or develop. Changing or developing means thinking about you, however modestly - your needs, goals, abilities, constraints, opportunities, situation, daydreams, fears, ambitions, responsibilities, feelings, loves, hates, and the rest.

'Stuckness' saps the vitality of organizations too. It is less easy to recognize than global competition, exchange rates or major change, it remains largely hidden until special circumstances bring out latent courage and energy and we amaze ourselves with what we can achieve. Stuck people are among the main causes of under-performance in organizations (the larger, the truer); people stuck in limited jobs or operating with limited levels of knowledge, skill or ability, people stuck with no vision, ambition or desire to do better any more. We call them variously bureaucrats, sleepers, demotivated, fed up, bored or lazy, timeservers, clock-watchers, skivers and a host of other names.

A manager in a large British public service organization described this situation as she experienced it:

How much can we continue to change? You see people hanging on, hanging on even at 48 or 49, to pension rights, security and so on. I think a lot of stress in middle management is caused by this. People go to ground, entrench and hide themselves, half-knowing they are not performing well, but hiding the evidence. I'm being told to rattle the sabre around them, but I think this will only make them worse. They're often nice people, gentle and kind, you can't call them in and tell them their work is no good. They need help, they're often doing their best in their own way and we don't have the resources to help.

It has started me thinking about my own career. I don't want to end up like this. Why is it that with some people the years just become increasingly painful for both them and for those around them, while others provide good models into their sixties and beyond - of changing themselves and helping people around them to change?

Whatever the cause, stuck people have switched off or limited their effort as far as their organization at least is concerned, and perhaps in the rest of their lives. Stuckness is not simply a problem of ageing - there are plenty of stuck twenty-five-year-olds and many eighty-year-olds still puzzling, enquiring and changing their minds. It is perilously easy to get stuck. Sometimes a sense of stuckness comes to a violent head. We hold our needs down, perhaps not even being fully conscious of them, until one day . . . whoosh!. . . there is an explosion, with lots of energy, excitement ... and casualties. Suddenly discovering these needs after years of repression can make us very angry, careless of a new strength, hurting and blaming those unfortunates within reach.

As managers and adults it is a vital part of our own development to review those childhood messages and principles that we have come to live by, and see how relevant they are to our current life situation. Is such-and-such behaviour a compulsion, an empty ritual, a way of avoiding upsetting someone whose anger I fear, or on whose favour or patronage I depend? Or is it indeed a useful, satisfying rule of conduct? For one of the key aspects of a healthy style of self-management is that I decide for myself whatever rules or customs are productive and appropriate, and then try to live by these - whether or not they fit current norms and expectations.

So managing me need not be a selfish pursuit, but a necessary force for life and health in people and organizations. When we get set in our ways, feel that 'we have arrived' or otherwise limit ourselves, we are contributing to the stuckness of everyone. We owe it to ourselves and to those around us not to deny and repress our needs, but to become more aware of them and to consider how they can be met, along with the needs of others. In breaking away from 'either my needs or yours' to 'what can we do to meet both your needs and mine?' - you may be saving more than just one life. Not getting stuck means surviving, maintaining and developing yourself. Like stuckness, enthusiasm is also contagious: it infects us and we infect others. The renewal of other people - in organizations, communities, even societies - depends on such enthusiasts.

2 Getting Things Done

In Chapter 1, we noted that managing yourself involves your identity, skills, health and action in the world. Since managing is about doing, we put action at the centre, and focus on this first. Table 2.1 on p.30 sets out the kind of inner processes involved in getting things done.

In subsequent chapters there are, amongst others, ideas about understanding and valuing yourself, how to identify your skills, and keep yourself fit - all things that - will help you take successful action. Because the focus is on action first, we look here at what is involved in moving from understanding and planning to doing. Though by no means all action is planned, a typical managerial sequence is as follows:

First, weigh up the circumstances:

- prioritize and clarify your aims or intentions

- generate alternative courses of action

- evaluate the alternative courses of action

- decide which course of action to take - i.e. make your resolutions

and then take action:

- plan what you are going to do - your first steps

- carrying out first steps - action

- review and plan next steps, and so on.

Aspects of the self that require managing	Inner processes that require managing		
	Thinking	Feeling	Willing or doing
Action in the world: getting things done	Ability to make your own decisions, for yourself, as well as being open to suggestions and feedback from others. Decisions made with an understanding of the way in which your actions affect other people, and have consequences for them as well as for you.	Concern both for your own interests and for those of other people - thus making moral decisions.	Going out and taking initiatives; courage. Managing and transforming setbacks, disappointments, frustration; determination.

Table 2.1: Action - Getting things done

At this point, stop and think about the way you set about taking action and turn to Activity 4 on p.176.

ACTIVITY 4 Page 176

PRIORITIZING : CLARIFYING YOUR INTENTIONS

There are many issues and questions about which you have to take decisions, make plans and take actions. Sometimes it is clear where to start, but often it is useful to take a slightly more systematic approach to priority setting. The first step in this process is to identify the questions coming your way.

Questions coming your way

By 'questions coming your way' we mean those things you need to do to survive, develop or maintain yourself. In each person's life there are many questions and issues. Some press on us all too clearly, others are there only if we look for them, and still others are just over the horizon - giving us the choice of proactively seeking them out or waiting, more reactively, until they hit us. Here are some examples:

- Work issues - connected with what's expected of me in my job or role that require better self-management, such as taking a risk or confronting a problem.

- Questions coming from other people - things others are saying to me or asking me; relationships that need changing one way or another; unfinished business with somebody.

- Questions arising from my life - past and future; throwing off burdens or hindrances from the past; recognizing positive things and seeing where they might lead; looking for opportunities, challenges, purpose in the future; coming to terms with getting older, and seeing what this means both in the way of limitations and of opportunities.

- Issues to do with me, my personality, the way I am; my stage of development, my health, skills, sense of identity; my style or mode of managing.

Just reading this list may give you an idea of some things to think about. However, the main purpose of this chapter is to examine ways of moving from an understanding of the issues into deciding what to do about them (intentions) and then planning action (resolutions) and carrying these out. This equips you to move into the action phase.

How you read this chapter will depend on where you are on these issues. You may not be sure what your questions are at the moment, and you might want to skip this chapter and return to it after some of the others. On the other hand if you are already aware of some questions or issues facing you, you can immediately try out the action process we are about to describe.

Getting an overview: domain mapping

Assuming, then, that you are aware of some questions and issues facing you, how do you prioritize them? Domain mapping is a technique that can help. Peter Ford, the personnel manager from Chapter 1, can provide us with a worked example of a domain map (Figure 2.1). The domain map consists of a series of rings, like a dartboard, with you at the centre - the bull's eye. The 'board' is divided up into a number of segments, or 'domains', one for each question or issue. In the first ring around the bull, you write in each segment a question or issue you are working on. You do this by considering your relationship with it, whether it is a relationship with a person or a task or even a part of yourself.

In the next ring, you write a brief description of how things are with each of those relationships or aspects of your life at present. Thus, Peter has identified five areas or 'relationships' that are currently causing him concern, and that require action if he is to manage himself more effectively:

- with colleagues - he is always pushing them, with no time for fun or relaxation

- with his temper - Peter loses it often, especially at home ('the children seem to be growing up fast without much help from him and since Sam returned to work . . .')

- with his lifestyle - he's always rushing about all over the place

- with his health ('headache . . . rheumatism')

- with his life's direction, a nagging doubt, only half-formed (or half-allowed?)

- about whether what he does is all that important ('What does it all add up to?')

Fig 2.1: Peter's domain map

In the third ring out, you write in how you would like that aspect or relationship to be. You can see in Figure 2.1 what Peter has written in for each. Already the picture so far gives an overview of your issues and questions, which can help you choose priorities and clarifying intentions. (We will return to the remaining rings later).

CLARIFYING INTENTIONS

Which issue(s) and which desired end result(s) are you going to work on? Choose one or two segments from the third ring away from the bull; these are your priorities that you can make into intentions. Sometimes it is hard to choose a priority. Although the choice must be yours, here are some of the criteria that you can use when making your decision:

- Which is the most important, which matters most? Is it the one you really want or need to tackle? Will have the biggest pay off for you and/or for others?

- Which will have the quickest pay off and show some results very soon? (You may be lucky in that the one with the biggest pay off is also the quickest, but often there is some trade off between speed and effect)

- Which can be said to be the most urgent, where the effects of not tackling it will be the most disastrous or will be felt soonest?

- Which will be the easiest to tackle? (start with an easy win?)

- Which will be the most difficult to tackle? (start with the big one; 'If I can handle that I can handle anything.')

- Is there a key issue, connected in some way with many of the others, or that working on this one will also lead to progress elsewhere; or that until this one is resolved, nothing much can be done about the others?

Peter Ford decides that his priority is to work on his lifestyle. This is because it is playing a significant part in causing some of his other difficulties, such as signs of stress illness, not seeing enough of his family, losing his temper and, to some extent, the unsatisfactory relationships with his colleagues. He realizes, though, that it will be some time before the effects of any changes here will be fully felt, and he wants to make an immediate start on improving his health. So these two are his clear intentions.

ALTERNATIVE COURSES OF ACTION

There are usually several alternative routes to any given goal. Much depends on the goal itself; sometimes, simple, clear-cut actions can be readily identified, but at other times the appropriate steps are not so easy to recognize.

In Peter Ford's case, his short-term intention to improve his health, particularly by working on his stress-related symptoms, is relatively straightforward. For example, he could:

- go to the doctor and get drugs (painkillers, tranquillizers)

- take up a sport - e.g. squash, which a lot of his colleagues play

- start a programme of physical fitness training

- start a programme of meditation

- start some combination of the above.

But with Peter's longer-term intention to change his lifestyle there are no simple techniques or prescriptions. When working on the bigger issues like this, there are four broad strategic choices:

1. Change the situation: confront Anne, with whom you are having a difficult time; demand that the Marketing Department gives you more notice of special promotions so as to give production more chance to handle the extra output; make improvements to the recruitment system and coach Richard in doing his job better, so that you are not burdened with picking up his mistakes.

2. Change yourself: perhaps Anne has a point - you are being unreasonable; you should be more available and open when

Marketing does try to discuss things with you; perhaps you want Richard to make mistakes, so that you can show how clever you are. You may need to examine and change your own behaviours and attitudes, perhaps take a different perspective, listen to others, acquire new skills or knowledge.

3. Leave the situation: find as constructive and positive a way of moving on as possible - constructive to you and, ideally, for all the others involved. At very least, try to minimize the destructive effects of your moving. Check that you are not jumping from the frying pan into the fire. Look out for signs of undischarged anger - 'I'll show them. I'll take all the forecasting data with me, so they'll have to go over it all again!'

4. Decide to live with the situation: but come to terms with it. Shrug your shoulders; say, 'You can't win them all'; make Elizabeth a less important part of your life - it's more her loss than yours; give in graciously; or persevere and give yourself rewards and treats for sticking with it. The important thing about deciding to live with it is that you don't continue to feel angry and resentful or moan and worry about the situation, and don't allow it to give you negative feelings about yourself or the other people involved. You move on, psychologically if not physically.

In considering these strategic choices, it is very helpful to have a partner or a group (as discussed in Chapter 7). They can give information, advice and also act as a sounding board for you to think aloud, bounce off ideas and receive feedback.

The way Peter's life is, it is not likely that he will think immediately of finding such a 'speaking partner'. So for the time being at any rate he will have to rely on his own ideas. However, as one of his concerns is his relationship with his family, could he not talk through his intention with his wife, Sam?

Sometimes it can be very difficult to explore issues thoroughly with the people who are closely involved in, and affected by, them. Because they are so involved it is almost impossible for them to be detached enough to look objectively at the pros and cons. Ideally, when listening to or counselling someone, if you are to be helpful you need to be able to enter that discussion in a free state where you are not looking to gain anything from that person. So, knowing this either consciously or subconsciously, Peter decides not to talk about this with Sam - not for the time being anyway. After some thought, he is able to generate four alternative strategies.

- Give up his job, become a house-parent and depend financially on Sam's earnings.

- Remain with the bank, but ask to be transferred to a less demanding job (i.e. seek voluntary demotion).

- Seek a less demanding job with another employer.

- Remain in the same job, but change his approach - e.g. delegate and trust others more, learn to say 'No', try to lessen his desire always to be in the forefront and the limelight.

On considering this fourth option, Peter realizes that it contains within it a new issue or a new aspect of the original - namely 'his desire always to be in the forefront, in the limelight'.

This illustration of the action process, although described in seven convenient linear steps, shows how it is often an untidy process, involving going back to earlier steps, modifying, then moving on again. 'Three steps forward, two steps backwards and one step sideways,' as our colleague Malcolm Leary puts it.

EVALUATING THE ALTERNATIVES: RESOLVING ON A COURSE OF ACTION

This entails weighing the advantages and disadvantages of each. There are two sets of pros and cons - in terms of practicability and in terms of likely effects. Practicability is about whether any given action is realistic, given the resources available, the possible obstructions or resistance, as well as the positive factors that will help. Separate from this is the question of likely effects or outcomes. Will the action achieve your goal? What are the possible side effects (negative and positive)? What will be the consequences for other people, as well as for you? Force field analysis is a useful technique for looking at these sorts of questions.

Force field analysis

Though it sounds rather complex and sophisticated, force field analysis is actually very simple and gives an overall picture of the helping and hindering factors related to any proposed course of action. Let's look at one of Peter Ford's alternatives for improving his health. It doesn't matter which one we take (and it might be helpful to do all of them), so we'll take the first - 'Go to the doctor for painkillers and tranquillizers'.

Figure 2.2 shows the start of the force field analysis. First draw a line, representing where you are now, with a big arrow upwards in the direction of where you want to be - aiming at your intention.

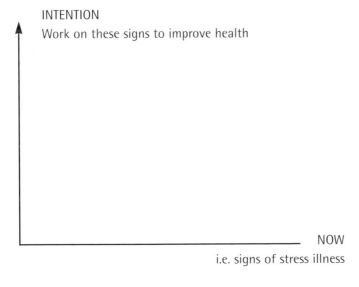

Figure 2.2: Force field analysis

Then take the course of action that you are considering, in this case option 1 of the 5 set out on p.36, and think about all of its pros and cons. Now draw these in on the diagram as arrows either pointing upwards (if it will help the action succeed, or downwards 'if it will resist or hinder the intended action'). You can vary the length of the arrows to show whether this force is relatively strong or weak.

Thus, in Figure 2.3, Peter thinks that the fact that going to the doctor will not help him with his intention to change his lifestyle outweighs the fact that it is easy; and the short-term effectiveness is outweighed by the probable long-term ineffectiveness.

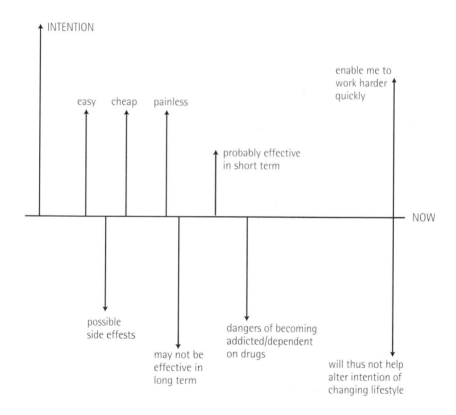

Fig 2.3: Force field analysis - Option 1

Similarly, we can do this type of analysis for each of the possible actions, for example, the fourth alternative, 'meditation' (Figure 2.4).

Comparing these figures it appears that, of these two, meditation is the better. An analysis for all his options leads Peter to his resolution: a combination of meditation and fitness. He abandons the idea of squash because it would take him out of the house even more and perhaps add to his competitiveness and desire to be in the lead, thus working strongly against his other intention. You will see that this resolution has been entered in the next ring on Peter's domain map (Figure 2.1).

This is, of course, a relatively simple intention to work on (though not necessarily to action). With more major changes or courses of action, other people are usually involved and this

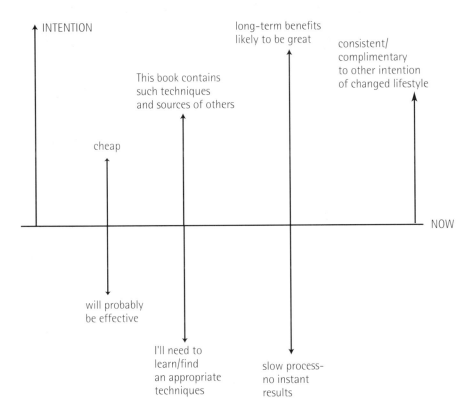

Fig 2.4: Force field analysis - Option 4

confronts us with the central paradox of managing me first - that although self-management is of great importance, it needs to be done in full consciousness of the effect of your actions on other people. In making a conscious choice, taking into account the effects on others, and then deciding what to do (rather than just drifting or being forced), you are behaving in a 'both ... and ...' way, aware and responsible for the consequences *both* for yourself *and* for others. The probable consequences of a particular action may be fairly clear, but often, especially with more complex issues and concerns, it is not simple; in such cases, some moral imagination is needed.

Moral imagination

'Moral imagination' is Rudolf Steiner's term for bringing to consciousness the consequences of your actions, both for yourself and for any other 'stakeholders' who are involved or affected by them, and therefore who have an interest or right to be considered. In the end it's your decision, but it will then be made in full consciousness of its effects. Of course, this often makes it harder to decide - but at the very least you might be able to consider ways of lessening the negative consequences for others, rather than just ignoring them or, in some ways worse still, being unaware of them. As ignorance is no defence in law, so in the moral sphere unawareness is no excuse.

Moral imagination is easier to describe than to do! It involves taking the possible course of action that you are evaluating, and imagining that you are now some time in the future, and that you did indeed make that particular choice. In other words, you have put that particular option into operation, and you are imagining what has happened as a result.

You will have to decide for yourself what time span to use; you could try several for a big decision - say one month, then six months, then one year. It is important to be as detailed as possible in your imagination; try to see what is happening, form a mental picture; look for details such as colours, sounds, smells. What are you thinking? How are you feeling? What are you wanting to do, and actually doing? Who else is involved? What is each of them thinking? How is each of them feeling? What is each of them doing?

Although this may seem quite difficult at first, it is worth persevering. It's surprising how you soon realize that something you thought was a good idea is not that good at all; or that you just haven't had enough information yet to make a proper choice or decision. Or that if you are to take such-and-such action, there are various other things you will need to do first; or you can do, to make it less unpleasant for some of the others involved.

For example, in the case of Peter Ford's intention to change his lifestyle, he soon realized that the option to stay at home and be a house-parent was not for him. In his imagination he saw himself feeling frustrated and bored; and anyway, after quite a short time-span the children had left home, so there was very little 'house-parenting' to do.

In fact, after doing force-field analyses and moral imaginings on the other alternatives, Peter came to his second resolution: to stay in his present job but change his attitude to it.

PLANNING FIRST STEPS

Many models of decision-making stress the importance of detailed action plans, which map out all the various steps that you are going to have to carry out, with target dates, criteria for measuring success, sub-plans for allocating resources, and so on. Our approach is slightly different, since we have found that action planning often becomes a convenient vehicle for avoiding actually doing anything.

Instead, we like to focus on the first step; what is the first thing you are going to do? Once you have carried out that step, you can think about the next one; and so on.

For Peter, his first resolution is relatively simple. He can start right now - or tomorrow evening - when he gets back from Edinburgh, when he will begin some of the exercises and meditations from Chapter 6 of this book. Even here, though, he needs to give a bit more thought to timing. Bearing in mind his desire to share more with his family, it would be a good idea to spend the evening telling Sam about his plan, rather than disappearing to do exercises and meditation. So he changes his mind - he'll start the day after tomorrow: the fitness exercises as soon as he gets home, and the meditation later in the evening, after dinner.

His other resolution is more complex. What opportunity is about to come along for him to start with his new attitude? Well, he can cancel that trip to Paris - ask Janet to go instead. She'll probably be delighted, if a bit nervous, and it will be quite a developmental opportunity for her - provided Peter briefs her fully. . . . Well, not *too* fully; she's got to be given the chance to think for herself, and he must start trusting her, along with the others.

With any first step it can be very useful to rehearse it. You can rehearse on your own - talking to yourself perhaps - but it is probably better to do it with a partner or in a group, perhaps with someone role-playing the other person. This helps clarify what you are going to say as well as building confidence and gaining the courage to get out there and say it. Another way of getting yourself ready psychologically is to use affirmations, 'I can do it'. This technique is explained in Chapter 4.

You can also make a 'telepathic contract' with your speaking partner or with members of your support group. This involves setting a time when you are going to carry out your first step, and the other agreeing to think of you at that time - sending you 'telepathic support vibrations' as it were. When we use this with development groups, receivers of telepathic support often say it has been extremely helpful, 'Knowing you were all thinking of me enabled me to go in and tell my boss I thought she was wrong.' Here is another way to prepare:

Visualization

First, get yourself relaxed (see Chapter 6 for a good relaxation exercise). Then choose the step or action that you are going to take.

Now imagine that you have taken the step; create a clear mental picture of you and/or the situation as you want it to be. Suppose, for example, your goal is to be able to address a large group without being overcome by nervousness, and that your first step will be to speak at the sales conference next week.

Now imagine yourself, poised and confident, standing in front of the group and giving a wonderful presentation. Try and be as detailed in your visualisation as possible; include the audience, and look at the way they are enjoying and admiring your performance. Revel in you ability to give brilliant answers to their questions. Hear and enjoy their applause. Bask in the glory of thanks and praise afterwards.

Does this sound a bit far-fetched? Well, try it. How many times has the opposite worked, where you have tortured yourself with images of failure only to find them coming true?

DOING AND REVIEWING

The most important thing to say about doing is - JDI! (Just Do It) Get on with it and carry out your first step. Easy to say isn't it? But what happens when your courage fails you or your willpower deserts you?

First remember your resolution and why this is important to you. If you did a rehearsal, remember what you learned from that. Then think of others who are supporting you - your speaking partner or support group. At one of our workshops a participant said that he felt he had to carry out his first step because he owed it to the group who had helped him come to his resolution; this had sustained him when otherwise his courage would have failed.

If you made a 'telepathic contract', then carry that with you -

sense the support coming your way. There are other sources of 'super-sensible' support too. If you have spiritual beliefs you may look to them for support and guidance. Or listen to an inner friend - that inner voice that will, if you allow it, tell you what to do and how to do it. How in touch with it are you? The backwards review in Chapter 3 and the meditation routine in Chapter 6 are exercises which help in getting in touch with this inner voice.

When you are taking your first step, try to be aware of yourself and what you are doing. Watch yourself objectively - as though you were watching someone else. Try to observe things like:

- *The Physical* How is this person (i.e. you)? Tense or relaxed? Still or fidgeting? Breathing shallow and rapid, or deep and slow? (We say, 'I took a deep breath and got on with it.')

- *Thinking* What are this person's thoughts, ideas and assumptions in this situation? Why? Where are they coming from? What effect are they having?

- *Feeling* How is this person feeling? Why? Where are these feelings coming from? What effect are they having?

- *Willing* What would this person like to say or do? Why? Where is this coming from? What is her motive? What does he really want to do? What is she in fact prepared to do? What effect is all this having?

As well as being aware of yourself, ideally it is best if you can become aware of what the other people involved are thinking, feeling and willing. We look at this in Chapter 7 in examining the ways you can work with others.

The reviewing process as we have described it actually starts during the doing. A fine balance is needed here between getting on with it and being aware of consequences. Too much observation might deflect you off course, too little might prevent you realizing when you are getting nowhere, or making things worse, so that a change of plan is indicated. Afterwards it will certainly be helpful to take a detached look at what happened, what you did, how you did it, what you can learn. Backwards review and critical incident analysis (Chapter 3) will both help here as well as talking it over with your speaking partner or support group.

Maybe you will see your resolution in a new light, or recognize other key issues, or domains for mapping out action. Make sure you are not simply shying away from the original purpose and don't be lulled by early success into thinking, 'That's it!' However crucial and important, this was but a first step. The aim of the review is to ready you for the next step, and so the cycle continues.

COURAGE AND WILLPOWER

Since courage and willpower are particularly important in action, you might want to try some strengthening exercises. Building courage and willpower is a bit like building muscles - the more you use them, the stronger they get. If something requires an effort of will to do it regularly - like many of the activities in this book - and you are able to keep doing it, then your willpower gets stronger.

Special willpower exercises

These are of two kinds - those requiring an effort of will actually to do at all; and those where the will comes in continuing to do them every day. Examples of the first kind are:

- When tempted to say something, don't.

- When you want to do something immediately, postpone it to a definite, specified time in the future.

- Conversely, when you want to postpone something, do it now.

- Do something that you know you don't want do; something simple, like not putting sugar in your tea, when you normally have it.

- Still on food, order something you've never had before but suspect you will dislike.

- Talk to one complete stranger every day for a week.

- In a restaurant ask for something that's not on the menu.

- Think of a situation you normally avoid and put yourself in it, complain (as constructively as possible) about poor service, or unsatisfactory goods.

- Wear bizarre clothes for a day.

The second kind involves setting yourself a daily task or routine - perhaps at the same time each day. The actual activity is not particularly important, the regularity and repetition is what builds up the will. Some examples are:

- going for a short walk

- keeping a diary of the weather or of any other daily occurrence

- doing one of the exercises everyday from this book - perhaps backwards review (in Chapter 3).

3 Knowing Yourself

In this chapter we turn to the core issue of identity. We have already noted that the four aspects of managing yourself - health, skills, action and identity - are closely interconnected, and it is clear that my sense of me, of myself, is very dependent on my health, skills and the things that I do. Table 3.1 on p.50 shows some aspects of identity discussed in Chapter 1.

KNOWING, VALUING AND BEING MYSELF

From early schooling we are taught about others, their actions and achievements, their ideas and theories, what they believe and what motivates them. There is often less encouragement to think about these things as they apply to ourselves, to find out about our own actions, achievements, strengths, weaknesses, effects on others and so on.

Sometimes we have been taught that other people know more than we do; that others are cleverer, better educated, more attractive, nicer people. This can result in us devaluing ourselves relative to others. But even when we are not being told these things by parents, teachers, bosses and other authority figures, it is all too easy for us to put ourselves down and to acquire a poor self-image, whenever we do something not as well as we would wish.

Pressures to conform come in many guises, some are fairly subtle. It is not surprising therefore that it can be quite a struggle to move towards trying to think, feel and act for ourselves. The research mentioned in Chapter 1 on the characteristics of effective managers suggests that they go through a number or stages of development in a direction of greater self-management. These stages or modes of managing are summarized below.

Aspects of the self that require managing	Inner processes that require managing		
	Thinking	Feeling	Willing or doing
Identity, self	Personal values, ethical and moral standards, and philosophical, spiritual and/or religious beliefs. Awareness and understanding of these and other aspects of self. Thinking about myself and knowing myself.	Recognizing my strengths and rejoicing in them; accepting myself in spite of my weaknesses. Valuing myself.	Self-motivation, purpose in life; sense of security faith and hope. Being myself.

Table 3.1: Aspects of identity

But before looking at these stages, think about where you are by completing the questionnaire in Activity 5 p.179.

THE FIVE MODES OF MANAGING

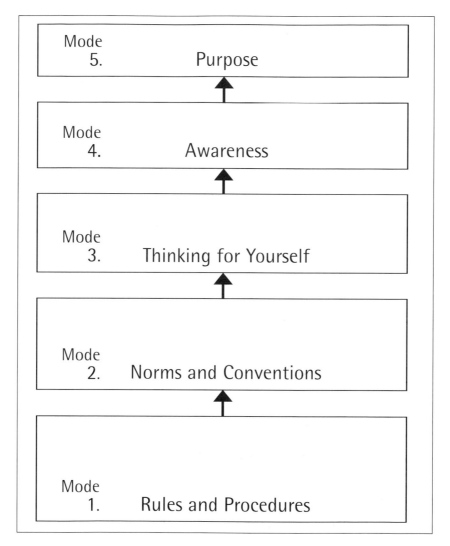

Figure 3.0: Five Modes of Managing

Developmental modes 1 and 2 are influenced mainly by external factors. In mode 3 internal factors have a big influence. In mode 4, it is both internal and external factors, in a synthesis of the two. In mode 5, you apply this synthesis, this art of managing yourself, to a particular purpose - to your purpose in life.

Developmental stage or mode 1: Rules and procedures

Benefits of this way of managing
Set procedures and so on can be of use in certain types of emergency, where it is particularly important to do the 'right' thing quickly and correctly. They are useful for beginners, because they can provide a reassuring base from which to start.

Effect of being blocked at stage 1
A few managers get stuck at this stage and can only operate in a limited number of 'standard' situations. They are likely to be ineffective at anything truly managerial.

Nature of next developmental step
To move on, you need to start querying, modifying or deviating from standard procedures, seeking explanations and reasons rather than mere instructions.

Developmental stage or mode 2: Norms and conventions

Benefits of this way of managing
Enables you to behave in an 'appropriate' way - in accord with accepted rationales and explanations that are socially and politically respectable. In so doing you are likely to be popular with authorities, keeping your nose clean and being considered safe, acceptable and reliable.

Effect of being blocked at stage 2
Many managers remain at this stage, and are quite happy to do so, since it can lead to a reasonably content existence. Yet such managers are likely to find any unexpected change most unpleasant and difficult to cope

with. Should they be forced to leave the organization (e.g. through redundancy) they tend to have a particularly bad time adjusting. Also of course, there is often a long-term price to be paid for not being oneself - a certain malaise, doubt, or 'surely there's more to life than this?' thoughts begin to creep in. They suffer from all the effects of not managing themselves that were outlined in Chapter 1 - i.e. they are stuck, become bored and lazy.

Nature of next developmental step

Start by questioning and challenging the established and accepted ways and reasons for doing things. Start to think for yourself; is this really the best way? Is this really a good, acceptable or valid explanation or reason? How can you find out for yourself and come to your own conclusion or decision?

Developmental stage or mode 3: Thinking for yourself

Benefits of this way of managing

Much more likely to be creative, and to be able to deal with new, ambiguous, changing situations, both within your organization and elsewhere in life. Also greater feelings of self-confidence and self-worth. The price to pay for this is that you may well be unpopular at times with those who like to maintain the status quo and do things in the 'proper' manner.

Effect of being blocked at stage 3

Being stuck at this stage means that you are so keen on thinking for yourself that you become too self-directing, completely ignoring the ideas, feelings, values and goals of other people, and the effect of your actions on them. Your confidence may distort into a form of arrogance.

Nature of next developmental step

To temper arrogance with humility and to combine self-management with management by and of other people; you need particularly to become aware of other views and of the effect of your actions on them before coming to your final decision. It is also useful at this stage to start thinking about what you have to offer others to contribute to their development.

Development stage or mode 4: Awareness

Benefits of this way of managing

Thinking for yourself, making your own decisions in full awareness both of yourself and of others and their goals, ideas, feelings leads to what is often seen as 'intuitive behaviour'. This involves 'both . . . and...' thinking, requires open-mindedness and suspension of judgement and, of course, this awareness enables you to choose which of these modes in which to operate. You now have a repertoire available from which to choose consciously. This is the stage of effective management, as outlined in Chapter 1.

Effect of being blocked at stage 4

Not a bad stage to be 'stuck' at! Yet there is a danger of abusing one's abilities and high level of consciousness to further personal ambition, manipulate others, gain power, or for other negative, even evil ends. You may now find an increasing desire to use your skills and ability to a particular purpose that you feel to be important.

Nature of next developmental step

Start to look for this special purpose; ask, 'Why on earth am I here? What am I doing with my life?'

Developmental stage or mode 5: Purpose

Now you are managing yourself with a full awareness of your purpose in life, of the task you want to achieve which in some way makes a definite contribution to the development of your organization, profession, area of expertise, community, affinity group, family, or whatever it is to which you choose to commit yourself. Even more here, there is the danger of a 'shadow side' to this commitment which can also serve negative or evil causes; this is where we find fanatics, despots and tyrants sometimes posing as saviours.

When people first become managers or take up any other new role, they are usually reasonably happy to obey the rules, use standard procedures, checklists and so on, as a secure basis from which to start (mode 1). After some time they become more aware and are able to work out the unwritten rules, norms, accepted practices, conventions, and explanations (mode 2).

Although quite a few managers are happy to stay in mode 2 - flowing with the tide and controlled by external factors - sooner or later those who go on to become more effective and achieve more, move on to the next stage of their development and add another mode of managing to their repertoire. Now they start to want to think for themselves and try out their own ideas to change things. Such people are more flexible, able to manage in times and situations of crisis and change.

Unfortunately, this may well bring them into conflict with those who prefer to stick to the established ways of behaving and doing things. Sometimes, the independent thinker's enthusiasm and self-confidence might get in the way of their objectivity, and a certain degree of arrogance can creep in. This needs to be tempered with humility, which comes from realizing that other people have legitimate ideas, opinions and rights.

As you get wiser - more aware - you learn to take a broader perspective. This will involve suspending judgement, keeping an open mind, listening to others, taking a 'both ... and ...' approach, getting feedback about yourself and your ideas, and considering the wider effects of your proposals, not only on yourself or your department, but also on others.

Although presented here as a clear progression, it's not always quite so easy to recognize your own - or someone else's - stage. For example, many managers become adept at recognizing the 'tricks of the trade' - the little things (like how not to show that you can't remember somebody's name) that really are somewhat manipulative. When carried out with consummate ease these may give the impression that the individual concerned is operating in a stage/mode 3 manner - having thought these things out for themselves. Really, however, this is not the case. For what we are seeing here is not true thinking, but an extremely subtle mixture of trial and error and ability to work out norms, i.e. operating somewhere between stage/modes 1 and 2.

This is the flavour of Dale Carnegie's *How to Win Friends and Influence People* and his 'one minute manager' approach which does not call for much thought (mode 3) or real human contact and empathy (mode 4). The popularity of these shows the desire of so many managers for something that will unstick them. But, if are you stuck at mode 1 or 2, a simplistic solution won't help in the long term and you will probably encounter plenty of '59 second employees' armed with a counteracting set of tips and tricks to stay ahead of the formulaic manager.

It is in mode 5 where people feel the need to use their maturity for a definite, identifiable purpose. Perhaps such people are in a minority; our research showed that most managers are normally operating between modes 2 and 3. A major aim of this book is to offer ways in which you can consider your own stage of development and take your next step.

Obviously it is now up to you to decide what you think of the five modes of managing and what you want to do about it. However, it is probably apparent by now that this book is intended at enabling you to increase your awareness, to move towards modes 4 and 5. It's not so much that mode 4 behaviour is always better than mode 1 or 2, but that the bigger your repertoire the more able you are to call on the one that seems most appropriate at any given time. To manage yourself effectively you need to be able to weigh up the situation, decide which mode to use, and go ahead in that way.

KNOWING YOURSELF

The ability to be effective as a manager or in life, however, rests on the even deeper foundations of one's sense of identity. In this account there are three aspects to identity - knowing, valuing and being yourself - and the rest of this chapter concentrates on the first of these.

Knowing yourself is a lifetime's work, and one in which we all ultimately fail, for no one can ever know everything about themselves. However if you have worked through this book so far you might already have a sense of increased self-knowledge, so you are even now moving in the spirit of 'knowing thyself'.

Receiving feedback constructively

There are various methods for increasing your self-knowledge.

Eliciting feedback from others is one of the most useful and Activity 6 on p.185 asks you consider occasions when this happened.

Feedback is one thing; responding to it is another. You may not like what you hear - negative information about oneself is never particularly pleasant to receive! As a result many of us tend to avoid opportunities for getting feedback. When we do receive information about ourselves that we don't like there are many ways of not accepting it. These include:

- denial ('It's not true')

- flight ('I must leave the room')

- rationalization ('It doesn't matter because . . . ')

- shifting the blame ('It was all because somebody else . . .')

- attacking the source ('That person's a fool anyway').

And also there are subtle combinations and other ways of dodging the issue. What's your favourite?

If you feel that the criticism is - or might be - justified, then try to listen; don't deny, attack or run away, but take the risk of drawing the person out, seeking clarification:

- 'Have there been other times when you felt that I insulted you?'

- 'Can you tell me more about just what it was I did that you found unacceptable?'

- 'Can you give me an example of the sort of behaviour you are talking about?'

- 'What was it I said that upset you?'

Figure 3.1 summarizes what tends to happen. How does this compare with your experiences?

Sometimes, of course, criticism is unjustified. Nonetheless, the person giving it to you must have some reason and if you want a continued relationship with them then it will pay you not simply to ignore or dismiss even unjustified feedback, but to clarify and tackle it.

To start with, it usually doesn't help to deny the criticism, nor to get on the defensive, nor to counter-criticize. Listen carefully, and try to see where the criticism is coming from. Is this the final result of something you did quite a long time ago? Or are you being blamed for somebody else, or because you are at the end of a long day of frustration, worry, feelings of threat, or whatever? If so, you will have to decide whether to let it pass or confront it, 'Look, are you worried about something? What's getting in the way here? What can we do together now that will improve things?'

Perhaps you can see why the other person feels as they do about you or what you have done, even though overall you don't agree with their interpretation or criticism. In a case like that, it's useful to show you do have some understanding - 'Perhaps I should have let you know sooner' or 'It could be that in my enthusiasm I acted too quickly and forgot to consult you.'

It is also very easy to receive positive feedback in a non-constructive way. Many of us refuse to hear good things about ourselves, and deny, trivialize or not really believe them. 'You're only saying that to be kind'. Learn to accept praise graciously - hear it, recognize it, acknowledge it: 'Yes, I am pleased with the way I was able to put my case' or 'Thank you, yes I think that I did do a good job that day.'

On the other hand, it's possible to be so taken with good news that you become smug, full of your own brilliance, and thus blind to other aspects of yourself. It is not uncommon to meet groups of people engaged in mutually sycophantic relationships, always giving each other unjustified praise, avoiding any form of potentially constructive criticism and development. A notable variant of this is the leader who surrounds him or herself with sycophants.

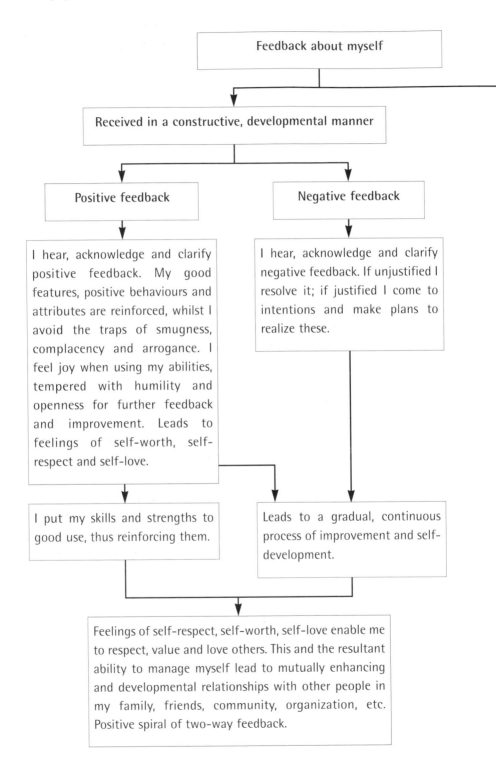

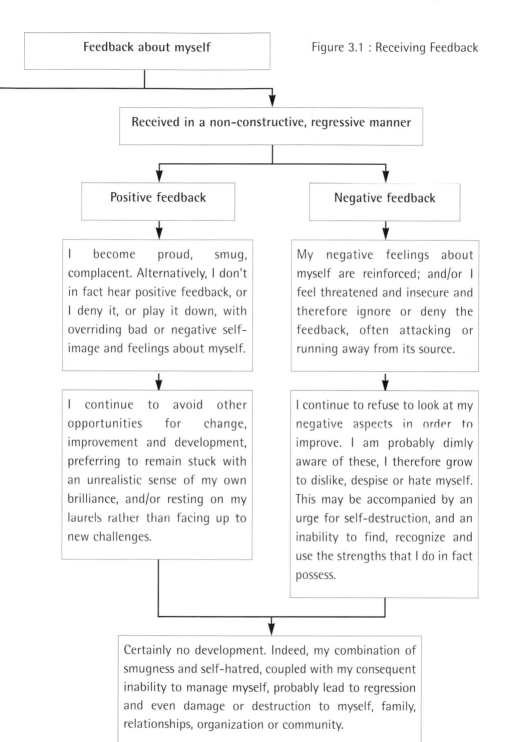

Figure 3.1 : Receiving Feedback

SELF-KNOWLEDGE EXERCISES

If you want to know, for example, how your hair is looking, you either use a mirror or ask someone. This, then, is the basic process of finding out about yourself: you need something, or somebody, to act as a mirror. Other people are so important in developing your ability to manage yourself that there is a whole chapter on it (Chapter 7). Here we will concentrate on other types of 'mirror'. But first of all, an exercise that actually requires the use of a real mirror.

Exercise: 'Mirror, Mirror on the Wall'

Sit or stand in front of a mirror - the longer it is, the better - with or without clothes on. Have a really good look at yourself - all too often we try not to see ourselves too carefully.

First, look at your physical self; how is your body looking? How do you feel about it? Ask various parts of it how they are getting on, what they would like from you, how they would like to be treated. Although this may sound a bit weird, give it a try - and allow time for you to 'hear' what they say. (Not that parts of your body can actually speak to you, but that usually we are so busy with noise and action that we just never hear what they are trying to tell us.)

Jot down your reactions so far. Then move on to think about your skills. Again, look in the mirror and say, 'This is a person who is skilful at............, and, it would be useful if he/she improved his/her skills at............' Again, jot down the answers.

Still looking at your reflection, think about what you do in the world. 'This is a person who has achieved............, and is currently doing, or about to do,............ Nonetheless, it would be helpful and useful if he/she were to get out and ....'.

Finally, 'What makes this person special is his/her............; as a result, he/she feels............ about him/herself.'

The purpose of the mirroring exercise is to get a better picture of yourself. However, you may well have triggered off feelings (positive or negative) about yourself; various ideas about exploring these are in Chapter 4. Don't forget, too, what we have said about planning and implementing action, back in Chapter 2.

Backwards review

This is a basic but fundamental exercise for becoming more aware and conscious of yourself, which you can do at any time, although towards the end of the day is the most logical.

Exercise: backwards review

Find a quiet place to sit (you can lie down, but it might send you to sleep; which might be good but it's not the purpose here!).

Go through the events of the day, in your imagination, starting with the most recent, and working backwards. Try to recall what you did; visualize this if you can - try to picture what happened. What were you thinking at the time? How were you feeling? What did you want to do? What actually did you do? And what of the other people involved - what were they thinking, feeling, willing and doing?

At first you will probably find this quite a difficult exercise. You could start by just going back over the past two or three hours, gradually extending it to cover the whole day. As a result you will gradually become much more conscious of yourself, how and why you behave, how you affect others, what effect they have on you.

Like a number of the activities and exercises in this book, backwards review works best when it is done every day over a long period of time (such as the rest of your life).

Critical incident analysis

A more occasional exercise is critical incident analysis. 'Critical incidents' are things that happen which have special significance for you; perhaps something you think you handled particularly well - or badly; perhaps when you felt hurt, or angry, or intrigued, or whatever. It's for you to decide. One way to analyse such critical incidents is through regularly writing up a personal journal.

Exercise: Keeping a personal journal

Take a notebook and divide the page into two halves, shown below.

Let a bit of time elapse (say at least a day) and then read over the incident again. How do you feel about it now? What do you think of it? What does it make you want to do? Is there any unfinished business? What have you learned from all this?

What happened	My behaviour
Note here what happened; who else was involved, what they did, and what you think they were feeling and thinking.	Write down your thoughts and feelings about this incident. What did you want to say and do? What did you actually say and do? (For a more detailed analysis you can use the self-observation questionnaire in Activity 4 on p.176.)

Over a period of time you may accumulate quite a number of incidents. You can then use another technique for interpreting them known as the Repertory Grid. This 'analytical mirror' is an excellent way of analysing data and looking deeper into information about yourself.

Exercise: Repertory grid

If, over a period of time, you have recorded, a number of critical incidents, and you have noticed a picture or pattern is emerging, you can explore this to find out more about what happens in those situations. As a first step pick out about ten incidents for analysis, say, half which you see as 'successful' ones, and half as 'unsuccessful'. So that it can be easily referred to, label each with a word or short phrase. As an illustration, here are six incidents from Tom's journal; simplified somewhat, but basically real happenings.

Synopsis of incident Label	Label
A terrible row in a shop, triggered off when they had sold out of something that had been widely advertised as on special offer.	Shop
A presentation to a group of managers to introduce them to the idea of joining a self-development group.	Presentation
A meeting with a sponsoring body to obtain funding for a proposed project.	Sponsor
An argument with the guard on a train because the buffet car that was shown in the timetable was not available due to 'operating reasons'.	Train
A lecture given to a group of management trainees.	Lecture
An altercation with a waitress in a restaurant because the allegedly 'fresh fruit salad' was from a tin.	Restaurant

When you have selected and labelled your incidents, draw up a chart as in Figure 3.2 entering the labels along the top row. The order doesn't matter.

Characteristics	Incidents					
	Lecture	Shop	Train	Restaurant	Presentation	Sponsor

Figure 3.2

Take each of the incidents and write its label on a separate small piece of paper, index cards are ideal. Shuffle these like a pack of cards and select any three of them at random; in the example given, this is three out of six, which are *Lecture, Train* and *Sponsor.* Take these three, and think about them in relation to each other. Now ask yourself, which two of the three are more similar to each other than the third; which two are in some ways alike, and which is the odd one out?

Here *Train* stands out as being different from the other two - it's the odd one out. Why is this? To start with it was handled badly, while the other two were handled well. This difference is then noted in the 'Characteristics' column, by making a small scale (or construct, to use the technical term) of 'Handled well *vs* Handled badly', like this:

L   R

Handled well   Handled badly

L and R stand for 'Right' and 'Left' and it doesn't matter which end of the scale you put the descriptions; they could be the other way round - whichever came to you first.

    Still considering these three, Tom notices that two are to do with work, whilst the other isn't. This gives the next construct:

L   R

Connected with work   Not connected with work

Continue this process until you can't see any other similarities/differences. Note that the pairings are not always the same; for example, using the same three incidents, Tom notices that the others involved in *Sponsor* are all older than him, while for *Lecture* and *Train* they are either younger or the same age. This gives the construct:

L   R

Other person(s) mostly older   Others mostly younger/same

Keep on working with the same three incidents, in various combinations of 2:1, until you have got out as many constructs as possible. Then return those three bits of paper to the pile, shuffle again, and select three more.

Suppose this time Tom comes up with *Restaurant, Presentation and Sponsor*. It doesn't matter that *Sponsor* has already come up - as long as all three are not the same. Immediately *Presentation* and *Sponsor* pair together on the already identified 'Handled well *vs* Handled badly' dimension. However, Tom also notices a new one, in that with both *Restaurant, Presentation* he was feeling quite ill with a cold, whereas with *Sponsor* he felt fighting fit. This adds another dimension:

L   R

Feeling ill at the time   Feeling well at the time

Continue this process until you have either gone through all possible combinations of the three-at-a-time incidents, and/or until you have a total of ten to fifteen constructs. In Tom's example, for brevity only the first six are illustrated. You should then have a chart looking like Figure 3.3.

What you now have is a list of incidents and a set of your own personal constructs - of the way you see things, think of them, perceive them. For example, there is an age factor in Tom's, even though at the time of the incident he was not conscious of this. At this stage it is worth looking at your list of characteristics or constructs to see what you make of them. Are there any surprises? Do they give you any ideas for doing something?

An interesting, though challenging, exercise is to select incidents that all involve the same other person or people, perhaps your boss, colleague or partner, and then either discuss your grid with that person or even work on it together. You may get some very useful insights by

Characteristics		Incidents					
		Lecture	Shop	Train	Restaurant	Presentation	Sponsor
L Handled well	R Handled badly						
L Connected with work	R Not connected with work						
L Other person(s) mostly older	R Others mostly younger/same						
L I was feeling ill at the time	R I was feeling well at the time						
L I felt cheated	R I did not feel cheated						
L I had set up the situation (power)	R The situation just arose (powerless)						

Figure 3.3

comparing your constructs for the shared incidents.

Your constructs, then, tell you not about how the world is, but about how you perceive it. You can take the exercise a stage further to see if you can find any insights into the way in which you respond to the world. In the example this is shown in Figure 3.4 on p.70.

Now each of the incidents has been 'scored' or 'rated' on each of the characteristics. So *Lecture* was seen by Tom as having been handled well (L on the first construct); connected with work (L); involving people not mostly older than him (R); he was feeling well (R); did not feel cheated (R); and he had set up the situation himself, thus feeling powerful in it (L).

Similarly, R or L are entered in all the other cases. (This is a very simple scale; some versions of repertory grids use numerical scaling, but these require computer analysis.)

Characteristics		Incidents					
		Lecture	Shop	Train	Restaurant	Presentation	Sponsor
L Handled well	R Handled badly	L	R	R	R	L	L
L Connected with work	R Not connected with work	L	R	R	R	L	L
L Other person(s) mostly older	R Others mostly younger/same	R	R	R	L	R	L
L I was feeling ill at the time	R I was feeling well at the time	R	R	R	L	L	R
L I felt cheated	R I did not feel cheated	R	L	L	L	R	R
L I had set up the situation (power)	R The situation just arose (powerless)	L	R	R	R	L	L

Figure 3.4

If you really don't think the construct applies at all to a particular incident, put an X to highlight that.

Finally, the analysis. What you are looking for is a pattern between rows in the grid. Before illustrating this, can you see anything emerging from the entries in Figure 3.4?

In this simple case there are a number of clear patterns, for example, the first two rows are identical:

L R R R L L
and
L R R R L L

In other words, from this data, it seems that Tom is much better (L) at handling things at work (L), since he handles badly (R) things not connected with work (R). An easy one to spot. Look now at the first dimension and the last-but-one - feeling cheated:

L R R R L L
and
R L L L R R

These two turn out to be exact opposites. However, as we said that it doesn't matter which end you put the various characteristics, if 'I felt cheated' had been at the R end instead of the L, then they would have been identical. Strange as it may seem, there is a perfect similarity between rows of exact opposites. So, in this case, Tom handled things well (L) when he did not feel cheated (R) (*Lecture; Presentation; Sponsor*). On the other hand, when he did feel cheated (L), he handled it badly (R) (*Shop; Train; Restaurant*).

Such a link does not in itself imply a cause. What Tom now has to do is to think about this carefully and decide if there is a 'message' there somewhere, and, if so, what it is and what, if anything, he wants to do about it.

Finally, let's compare the 'Handled well/badly' and 'Feeling ill/well' dimensions:

L R R R L L
and
R R R L L R

There doesn't seem much pattern here; L is paired with R three times, R with R twice, L with L once. It looks quite random, so at the moment, anyway, there does not seem to be any relationship between how Tom handles things and how well he is feeling.

The repertory grid provides a powerful tool for analysing your critical incidents and for gaining insight into the way you see, feel and respond to many circumstances. Note that instead of critical incidents you could have analysed people whom you like and do not like (writing their names across the top, and various aspects of them as the constructs); or things you like/dislike (or find easy/difficult) about your job. In all cases, finding a pattern can be a first step in taking decisions and acting to improve things.

Knowing yourself questionnaire

As one of the most common methods of getting information about people, questionnaires can be used as a means of gaining self-knowledge. Open-ended questionnaires can be used as an interview or discussion guideline, with you and the person you want to consult, asking each other the questions and discussing them as you go along. Because open-ended questionnaires produce open-ended answers that need interpretation, some people assume this requires an expert. Yet, in our philosophy of self-management, it is both possible and desirable for you to think about and interpret your own answers to such questions. In these circumstances it helps a great deal to discuss these with a friend or colleague.

To close this chapter, we offer an Activity on p.186 that requires answering a questionnaire on the theme of knowing yourself. This activity contains some tough questions but if you can find a good way of working with some or all of them - on your own, with a partner or perhaps in a group - they could well take you a long way down the road to knowing yourself.

4 Valuing and Being Yourself

This chapter continues the exploration of self-identity, by moving on from knowing yourself and on to valuing and being yourself. How do you value yourself at this point in your life? **As a start to this chapter, try the open-ended questions in Activity 8 on p.189 either on you own or with a 'speaking partner'** (see Chapter 7).

A **ACTIVITY 8** Page 189

DEALING WITH NEGATIVITY

In Chapter 3, we commented on the way that people can develop bad feelings about themselves as a result of negative feedback, or by making comparisons with others who seem much more competent, clever, beautiful, or whatever. These bad feelings spill over into our lives in two ways. They create a self-fulfilling prophecy; since 'I'm no good, no one will like me', I avoid others, withdraw, put people off, so indeed they leave me alone, because I'm not exactly the life and soul of the party.

Things can then get worse, because even though part of me is telling me I'm no good, another part doesn't want to believe that. So instead of taking responsibility for the fact that it's my own behaviour that is causing people to ignore me, I blame them - it's because they are nasty, or stupid, or boring, or whatever.

So they're not the sort of people I want to get on with anyway, and I'm better off ignoring and avoiding them. And so the vicious circle continues. The others notice my standoffish behaviour, and are all the more likely to keep away, reinforcing both my negative view of myself and my rationalized negative view of them. And so on and so on.

This pattern of behaviour is so common that there is a whole approach to psychotherapy based on understanding its more severe consequences. 'Rational emotive therapy' (RET) was developed by Albert Ellis, an American psychiatrist, who worked with patients who were very depressed and/or self-destructive. We do not suggest that 'the thinking manager', for whom this book is intended, is in need of therapy. But the principles of RET can be modified to help break these vicious circles that lead all of us at times to feel down, somewhat depressed, as though it's been a really bad day.

Ellis suggests that all people have a tendency to hold certain beliefs or assumptions about themselves and others that are irrational - there is no logical reason to hold them. One such belief - particularly prevalent amongst managers - is 'I should be perfectly competent in all respects.' Who says so? Where does this belief come from? As soon as you start to look at it you see that it is completely unreasonable. Nobody could possibly live up to it - even if our parents, teachers, bosses try to tell us it's true. Yet as long as we hold to that assumption we are going to be unhappy quite often, since there are bound to be many occasions when our lack of total competence becomes clear.

The trouble is, we then start the pernicious process of labeling ourselves. Not, 'Oh well, I would like to have done that better, but at least I can learn from it', but rather it is the label 'I am an incompetent person'. That vicious cycle again. How is it possible to throw off the label? Start by recognizing that the assumption behind it is nonsensical, and replace it with a much more sensible belief.

Replacing irrational assumptions

'I must be perfectly competent in all respects'

No-one can be perfectly competent in all respects. The holders of this vehicle for self-torture experience daily evidence that they are not such paragons of skilful virtue when they fail to live up to this impossible ideal. Consequently, they punish themselves, put themselves down, feel inadequate and, worse still, label themselves: 'I am a failure'; 'I am useless'. Things get so bad that even when they do something well, they don't recognize it. They feel they should have done even better. Or when someone gives them positive feedback, they don't hear it, or think, 'You're only saying that to be kind' or 'I was just lucky'. If you recognize this kind of negativity in yourself, you could work on replacing these messages, as follows.

'Nobody is perfectly competent at anything, let alone everything. However, like everyone else, I do have certain abilities, and can do certain things reasonably well.'

- List here all the things you are indeed good at. Overcome any false modesty - which is actually one of your inner enemies trying to stop you from valuing yourself. You could talk to others about this; perhaps even agree to work with them seriously on ways of managing yourselves (see Chapter 7) and you will soon overcome any embarrassment at asking others what you are good at.

'Of course, at times I will perform better than at others. However, these less successful times are not failures - but opportunities for looking at what happened and learning from it. Therefore I am not a failure - I am someone who is developing and learning to manage myself even more effectively.'

At this point you may find it helpful to strengthen the power of this new, positive assumption about yourself and the world by using the 'affirmation method' discussed later in this chapter.

'I must have the love and approval of others at all times'

Here is another guarantee of misery. To begin with, what wins the approval of one person is quite likely to be disapproved of by someone else, so either you live in a state of tension, on an emotional tightrope, or you are going to do things which some people won't approve of. In any case, if your behaviour is dictated by needs for approval, you're not exactly managing yourself, are you?

In the case of love, this is even more true. You can never be yourself if you are always doing things either to 'win' love or to avoid 'losing' it; and anyway, deep inside you know love is not a commodity like that. So your attempts to win or buy it will not succeed, but your irrational assumption triggers off another of your inner enemies and tells you that, 'There is something terribly wrong with me' and gives you a new label: 'I am unattractive'; 'I am unlovable'; 'I am horrible'.

So this is another negative cycle of self-fulfilling prophecy, which actually makes your behaviour less attractive to others, so they do find it harder to like you, thus reinforcing your view of yourself as unlovable, and so dismally on. At the same time, another neat device that your inner enemy employs is to make you blame it all on others. It is they who are unkind, uncaring, rejecting, unfair, and so on. Then there is the defence of rationalization: 'Those people are so boring, stupid, unattractive, wicked. . . . that I actually don't want them to like me anyway.' If you are familiar with this kind of negativity, you could work on a replacement as follows.

> 'It's nice when people like or approve of me but there are bound to be times when they won't. So what? Does it really matter? What is more important, managing myself or doing things to win friendship? If they don't want to be friends with me, so be it. In fact, lots of people do like, love or respect me.'

- Now list those people who do like, love or respect you. What sort of people are they? What sort of a person must you be if people such as them actually admire, respect, like or love you? What is it about you that they like? Can you check that out with some of them?

'Furthermore, people who don't seem to like me are not bad, horrid or whatever. It takes all sorts to make the world.'

This may well be another good time to use the affirmation method, which we'll look at later.

I have a right to rely on others to give me what I want

Nonsense! Not only have you no such right, but this belief is the very antithesis of self-management. Since you are not going to get everything you want from others, you will become disappointed, frustrated, angry with these other people who won't 'cooperate'. So you tell yourself that 'I am unlucky'; 'I am alone and helpless'; 'I am betrayed'; and you label everyone else as uncaring, unhelpful, selfish. A more constructive view is as follows.

'There will be many times when others can't, won't, or indeed should not give me what I want. So what? I have no right to expect this; after all they can't always expect me to give them what they want. In any case, it is not healthy to be so dependent. A mature person knows when to manage for themselves, when to seek assistance, and how to cope if help is not forthcoming.'

'Of course, it's nice to know that there are times when I can turn to certain people and ask for help - knowing that they will do their best but that if they can't help they will feel free to say so and we will still remain on good terms.'

- Now list such people and think about your relationship with them. What sort of demands do you make? Are these always reasonable? How do you feel when they are met or not met? What contributions do you make to their lives?

'People who can't or won't help or give me what I want have every right not to do so. They have their own lives to manage, their own pressures, deadlines, concerns.'

My inheritance, upbringing, and other things from the past determine my feelings and behaviour.

In other words, it is all somebody else's fault, and there is nothing I can do about it; so there is no point even trying. 'I am and always will be stuck - unskilful, unattractive, stupid, alone. 'I cannot ever change or do anything about it.' This is certainly a good one for getting you into a state of frustrated, depressed apathy - often combined with an envy or jealousy of others who appear to have had an easy time of it. Yet what about all those people who have overcome disabilities or setbacks? If you recognize this, you could work on replacing the message with the following.

'What I was born with, together with my upbringing and other experiences, have certainly contributed to who I am now. However, I am not stuck with this; I can change and develop and I am free to make what I can of myself. I can build on my strengths. I can develop a sense of meaning from my life so far by remembering the good things and transcending the unfortunate ones, by saying, "So what?" to them. And I can face up to the challenge of the life questions now coming my way.'

- Now list some of the more fortunate aspects of your life and identify some of the current challenges coming your way. A useful way of exploring this in more depth is the biography approach, explained later in this chapter.

> Incidentally, if you start to work with others and share biographies, you usually discover that people you think are so much better off have had their own problems and issues, some of which may put yours in the shade.

Unhappiness is externally controlled

Perhaps this is the core irrational assumption. As long as you blame others, project your feelings on to them, punish them - and yourself - for your inability to take charge of yourself, then you will remain stuck, blocked, unfulfilled and unfulfilling. Try this:

> *'Life is not perfect. However, I do have power and freedom to choose from four positive options to respond to difficult situations. I can choose to...*
>
> • Change the situation
>
> • Change myself
>
> • Leave the situation
>
> • Decide to live with the situation.

These are just some of the irrational assumptions or attitudes towards life that can hinder you in managing yourself. Do they sound familiar? If so, can you find a friend - either another person or an inner friend (a counterpart to the inner enemy whispering these destructive attitudes in your ear)?

HIGHER AND LOWER SELVES

Inner friends and inner enemies

We have encountered these already: in Chapter 1 Peter Ford's inner friend was telling him why he was taking on too much; his painful neck was a sort of message from within, saying, 'Hold on, start to look after yourself better.' He is aware of a part of himself - the fighting, politicking inner enemy, who doesn't want him to take stock of himself and what he's doing - that he doesn't like very much. In Chapter 2, Peter managed to listen to these messages, turn them into resolutions, and do something about them.

Chapter 3 shows two ways of receiving feedback - constructively and destructively - and here again the inner friend and enemy are at work. These inner beings are known as 'higher and lower selves' in anthroposophical psychology and each of us has both. Our higher self - the inner friend - tries to give information, feedback and other messages to enable us to do what is right, to make the best decision, to find courage when needed. This principle is recognized in various forms of development; in sports coaching it is known as the 'inner game', whilst meditation practices help us to listen to the subconscious, inner voice of our higher self. (For really skilled behaviour some of the 'super senses' are necessary - see Chapter 5.)

All too often though, the lower self - our inner enemy - seems to speak more loudly. It is so much easier to run away from a necessary confrontation; to shout and counterattack rather than ponder the validity of the other person's point of view; to wait until tomorrow before giving up smoking.

Becoming aware of both your higher and lower selves is a key aspect of knowing, valuing and being yourself. Your inner friend can help you to manage yourself in a positive and constructive manner but you also need to recognize your lower self, and try to deal with it. There are various strategies for this, depending on the nature of the beast. For example, some are very vulnerable to even being seen or recognized, so that merely identifying it - giving it a name, if you like - is sufficient to rob it of its powers.

Others thrive on your fear of them and as long as you are afraid of that part of you, or hate it (and hence yourself), they will get stronger. But they cannot live with being ignored or laughed at. When they pop up you need to say, 'sorry, not this time', and turn your back on them. Easier said than done of course, so perhaps you need the support of others in this (Chapter 7).

There are many fairy stories about monsters, frogs, beasts and so on that were transformed into princes or princesses by somebody who was able to overlook their hideous or frightening aspect and feel warmth, affection or love for them. The same is true of some types of inner enemy, since within them hides a positive quality, if it could only be released. For example, the inner spoilt child, who flies into a tantrum or sulks when she doesn't get what she wants, may also have other delightful childlike qualities, such as a sense of playfulness and wanting to be allowed into the world. Or the bore who goes on endlessly about his past experiences may, with some feedback and encouragement, become an interesting and entertaining raconteur.

The same is true of our higher selves, which often have a less pleasant side; wit can descend into hurtful sarcasm, courage betray us into foolhardiness and commitment harden into fanaticism.

EXERCISES FOR RECOGNIZING OUR HIGHER AND LOWER SELVES

It isn't too difficult to identify some of your inner friends and enemies because we are often vaguely aware of them. Try to recall a number of occasions when either your higher or your lower self, or both as is often the case, were in evidence.

If such occasions do not spring to mind, your critical incident diary will give you some clues, especially if you do a repertory grid (Chapter 3); if you can identify aspects of both your lower and higher selves, you could also try a repertory grid to analyse these further by using episodes when each was brought out as incidents. This will probably give you a lot of insight into the nature of these parts, when they are triggered off, who strengthens them, what weakens them, and so on. You might also like to try the following visualization exercise.

Visualization exercise I

Get yourself focused by reading through some of your critical incidents, or thinking about some of your personal traits and characteristics.

Then close your eyes, and imagine that you are looking at a blank cinema screen. Allow an image to form on the screen - an image of part of your inner self, an aspect of your higher or lower self.

This image may take the form of a person, an animal or bird, another type of creature or an object of some sort. Whatever it is, don't interfere in any way; simply allow it to take shape. It may change its form of its own accord; that's fine, as long as you are not changing it yourself.

Then allow it to speak to you. Listen to what it is saying. Can you sense what it is thinking? Or what it is feeling? Or what it wants from life - what is its ambition? Above all, what does it want from you?

If you cannot sense these, then ask it. And, finally, ask it its name. Then let it fade away.

This is a very difficult exercise for some people; perhaps no image appears at all, or you can't make any sense of what you do see. If that happens, don't worry; either forget it (some things will work for you; some won't) or think about it and try again later. For others this can be a very powerful experience, which you may find disturbing; so it is a good idea to do this exercise with someone else - either in pairs or in small groups.

If you did get an image - or a series, if you repeat the exercise over a period of time - you might wish to go further with the next exercise.

Visualization exercise II

Choose one of the aspects of your inner self to work on more deeply.

Close your eyes, and imagine that you are standing with it in a field. In the distance is a range of mountains, and you set off to climb one of these, with your inner being as your companion.

As you make your journey, the terrain changes. Sometimes it is rocky and steep; at others there are grassy plateaux, with birds and flowers. Sometimes it is warm and pleasant; at others times it gets cold, rains or snows, fog and mist close down.

As these things happen, observe your companion. How does she/he/it react to the different conditions? What does it do or say?

When you get to the top of the mountain, the view is breathtaking and the sun comes out bathing you and your companion in warm, golden light.

What happens now? How do you both feel about each other? What do you both want to do? What are *you* going to do?

THE AFFIRMATION APPROACH

One of the dangers of holding negative views of oneself is that it can lead to a self-fulfilling prophecy. In Chapter 1, Marion saw herself as being no good at interviews, and went on to perform badly. Yet the self-fulfilling prophecy can also work for good by starting off with positive views of oneself and creating a strong cycle where this is reinforced. This works even if you do not start with a very positive view.

The affirmation method was invented by the Frenchman Emile Coue in the early twentieth century; he called it 'autosuggestion'. There are a number of variants, but the principle is simple: decide on the positive view of yourself that you would like to be true, and then tell yourself, many times, that it is true. Coue's belief was that just as telling yourself 'I can't do such-and-such' leads inexorably to failure, so telling yourself that you can do it leads to success. Coue's famous affirmation, around which he built a highly effective therapy practice, was simply: 'Every day, in every way, I'm getting better and better.' If that sounds too good to be true, you may be right. Like any other approach, affirmation needs certain conditions to work properly.

Using the affirmation method

In moments of crisis, it is possible to use a quick, instant affirmation: 'Yes, I can do this'- but the method really requires regular disciplined application, ideally on a daily basis. To know what sort of affirmation you are going to make, you need to decide on the goal - what aspect of yourself or your life you want to improve.

This can be anything you want it to be: accomplish a specific task; have a better relationship with someone; be more healthy (but be precise - what aspect of your health do you want to improve?); feel good about yourself; and so on. Once you have a goal, various affirmation techniques are available. Here is one of them:

Affirmation exercise

Janet's goal is to feel better about herself - to increase her self-esteem. Using a notebook, or a few blank filing cards, she writes out the following:

'I, Janet, am more and more pleasing to myself every day.
You, Janet, are more and more pleasing to yourself every day.
She, Janet, is more and more pleasing to herself every day.

I, Janet, am beginning to like myself as a woman.
You, Janet, are beginning to like yourself as a woman.
She, Janet, is beginning to like herself as a woman.'

In each case, she writes it out three times, in the first, second and third persons, because our current views of ourselves are usually formed by a mixture of what we tell ourselves, what others tell us, and what others say about us.

Affirmations are always written in a positive sense so there are no negatives - not 'I am not tense any more' - but 'I am relaxed'. To try this method, write in your own name and use the same three-part formation as above on these sorts of basic statements:

I, ..., am beautiful and lovable.

I, ..., am talented, intelligent and creative.

I, ..., am growing cleverer every day.

I, ..., have much to offer, and others recognize this.

I, ..., am getting slimmer every day.

I, ..., am getting on better with ...... every day.

I, ..., have a really beautiful nose.

I, ..., have a lovely sense of humour that others appreciate very much.

I, ..., am beginning to forgive ...... for ....

I, ..., am getting over my disappointment at ....

I, ..., am working on that report so that it will be finished by ....

I, ..., am confident and can speak my mind clearly and confidently at meetings.

I, ..., am becoming nicer every day.

I, ..., am becoming happier to be me every day.

You can be as specific as you like. Create your own statements to suit your purpose. Write them out, putting in your name, and the names of anyone else involved, using I, you, she/he, at least ten times, and then read them out loud.

Alternatively, you can read your affirmations into a tape recorder and play them in your car, in bed at night, or indeed to wake you up in the morning; what a splendid way to start the day, hearing something wonderful being said about you!

As with many exercises in this book, you can also do this with a partner. This may be difficult at first, because we don't normally go around saying nice things about ourselves to others, but a partner can offer feedback about your affirmation and whether or not it sounds as though you mean it. Keep at it until you do mean it. If you feel a bit sceptical about this, fair enough, it's up to you what you experiment with. However, you could start with: 'I, ..., am open-minded and prepared to give this method a try!'

FAITH, HOPE AND SECURITY

If you experience your life as a random set of events, buffeted by whatever forces happen along, it is hard to manage yourself. A reasonable sense of faith, security and hope is necessary. What is meant by these terms? They often relate to the way you feel about the past and the future. Has the past left you feeling reasonably secure, in yourself, your relationships, your job? Or, as a result of things that have happened, do you have a general feeling of insecurity or isolation, of being different from others who seem to be able to cope much better, whose lives appear much kinder to them? Similarly, when peering into the future can you see the shadow of some horrible uncertainty looming? Or do you look forward with confidence, in faith that, whatever comes along within reason, you have resources within you or around you to cope or manage the situation?

Most people fall somewhere between these extremes; with some degree of security, faith and hope, but perhaps not as much as they would like. Perhaps the way you feel varies according to your mood and the circumstances? If you have used some of the methods elsewhere in this book, for example, backwards review or critical incidents and repertory grids (Chapter 3) you will already have a picture which suggests which situations, people and events tend to affect your feelings of security, faith and hope. Perhaps some of your unhelpful feelings are the result of the 'irrational assumptions' discussed earlier? Once you understand what is happening and why, you are more likely to be able to summon up your higher self to tame your insecurities.

In tackling this, there is no doubt that working with others, either as a pair or in a group (Chapter 7), can be of enormous help in seeking to increase your security, faith and hope. The very process of listening to others, sharing your concerns, getting things off your chest, discovering that others have had similar experiences, discovering friends, allies, contacts and comrades, can be enormously strengthening.

If, despite these ways of working on your ups and downs, you still feel low on faith, hope and security, some biography work may be helpful. This helps you look at past events and themes, and how they are affecting the present, before moving on, with increased sense of meaning and purpose, to examine the life questions facing you in the future. Again, though you can work on your biography alone, you are likely to get much more from the process by doing it together with a partner, or, ideally, with a small group.

Biography exercise

Here is a seven-step process for creating an overview of your life; working from the past, through the present questions coming your way now, in a way which enables you to make purposeful decisions about the future.

Step 1: Events

This first stage in biography work is a bit like backwards review, except that here you look back over the whole of your life so far, identifying incidents that stand out. Start in the present and think back over your life. What are the main events, turning points, landmarks or happenings that you can recall? These might be things which happened very quickly, and were short in time, or they might have taken place over quite a long period, and yet still be recognizable to you as a specific happening. Identify and write these events down. Obviously these will only be some of your life events - the ones most significant to you.

Now draw your 'life-map' on a large piece of paper - the larger the better - and going back in time as far as you want. The bottom edge of the paper is a time axis. How you picture or draw the events against time is up to you.

One common method is to make a graph or life-line by

plotting your events in terms of your feelings now or then - on some qualitative scale such as 'dreadful-to-wonderful', as below in Figure 4.1.

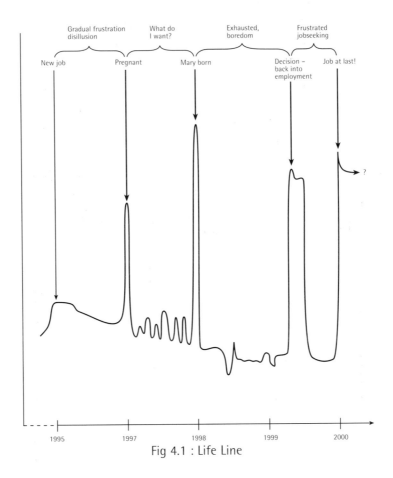

Fig 4.1 : Life Line

An alternative is to construct a collage of your life, using pictures and words cut from newspapers and magazines to illustrate or symbolize your life at particular times. If you are working with a partner or group, take time to share and discuss your events.

Step 2 : Periods

The next step involves looking at the spaces between your events and giving these descriptions. Figure 4.1 shows some examples; can you identify the periods between your key events? Give them each a name or label - you can use song titles or book chapters if you wish to come up with more imaginative names than ours. As before, share and discuss these with your partner(s).

Step 3 : Themes

Now look over your events and periods and see what themes you can recognize. A theme is:

- a recurring pattern - of thoughts, feelings, behaviour, occurrences

- a constant feature of your life - or a recurring feature present from time to time

- a tendency for certain things to happen

- certain aspects of yourself - including both your higher and lower self - making themselves apparent.

Here are some themes that often crop up in biographies:

- a tendency to undervalue myself

- recurring periods of ill-health

- travel abroad

- a pattern of problems when working with the other gender

- conflict between my responsibilities as a mother and what seems to be expected of me at work

- a very strong tendency to put myself second - to give way to other people's needs and ignore my own

- fear of new and unknown situations

- close family ties

- a strong tendency to be so independent that I will never do anything that anyone else suggests I do

- the 'spoilt child' in me - the way I react when I don't get my own way

- initiating things, starting them off, for others to take up and complete.

However, these are only indicative; it is your themes that are important. Sometimes they can be hard to spot and, if you are working with other people, they can be extremely helpful in asking questions and offering feedback about themes they think they might have spotted underlying your events and periods.

Step 4 : Questions coming my way

Step 4 is the pivot point of the biography process - it focuses on the now, the present - when the key events, periods and themes from the past have been considered, whilst future intentions and actions lie ahead. From what you have done so far, here are three ways to highlight the life questions facing you now.

(i) *Themes.* Consider your life themes. They can often be a good indicator of questions that need to be faced. What do your themes seem to be telling you? What are your thoughts about them? Can you recognize any patterns, for example:

- Have some themes disappeared from your life?

- Have some only just appeared?

- Do some come and go? If so, is there any pattern, or any set of causes, for this?

How do you feel about your themes, and their patterns? What are they saying? Are they pointing to any decisions or choices that you need to make?

(ii) *People in your consciousness.* Your events, periods and themes no doubt involved a lot of other people. Some of these will be part of your everyday life whilst others may be more distant, indeed, you may not have seen them, or thought about them, for years. Some may be dead; or not yet alive (e.g. a child you are currently carrying, or could never have). Yet, all of these are part of the network of people you carry around in your head or heart.

These members of your 'consciousness-net' are usually a telling source of questions. Take each in turn; although do not overload yourself, perhaps choose just one or two to start with.

What are your thoughts, ideas, beliefs about this person? How do you feel about her? And her being in your consciousness? What is he saying to you? What questions, decisions or choices are coming my way through or because of him?

You might also want to think about people who do not seem to be in your consciousness. What is this telling you or asking you?

(iii) *The overall picture of your life.* Imagine that your biography is that of another person - who has been describing it to you. What are your thoughts about this story? What are your feelings? What does that person need to face up to? What decisions or choices do they need to take? What unfinished business do you see? What are they achieving with their life? What remains to be achieved? Now, remember that 'they' is you. What is this biography saying to you?

Steps 5, 6 and 7 : Intentions, resolutions and actions
The aim of Step 4 is to find the important questions coming your way. Once these have been identified you can move and try to respond to those questions in the form of intentions, plans and actions.

Because of the design of this book, in starting with action we have already looked at the last three steps of the biography process in Chapter 2; if you have completed Step 4 and arrived at some important questions you can enter the prioritizing and decision-making process now.

5 Being Skilful

Skills are the way we translate our awareness into action. As it is the ability to do something well as a result of practice, a skill cannot be separated from the awareness that makes it possible nor the action that displays its performance:

> "He sparks the torch, and sets a tiny little blue flame and then, it's hard to describe, actually dances the torch and the rod in separate little rhythms over the thin metal sheet, the whole spot a uniform luminous orange-yellow, dropping the torch and the filter-rod down at the exact moment and then removing them. No holes. You can hardly see the weld. 'That's beautiful' I say. I'm bullshitting him. Who appreciates work like this anymore?"
>
> (Pirsig, RM *Zen and the Art of Motorcycle Maintenance*)

In this chapter we build upon the self-knowledge and awareness which form the focus of Chapters 3 and 4 by providing a framework for developing skills to help you manage yourself more effectively.

WHAT ARE SKILLS?

Skills are learned qualities which belong to the individual and not to organizations or employers. Skills are personal qualities. All people possess them and they are part of each person's identity. Given a supportive learning environment, skills can be enjoyable to acquire and deeply satisfying to practise. Because skilled action displays control and confidence, few things are more healing and satisfying to us, however simple, domestic and mundane. Making pastry, writing a letter in italic script, digging, even sweeping, washing up and scrubbing floors, can be highly enjoyable performances (a long as you don't have to do them all and every day at someone else's command).

Doing things well requires competence, good timing and an appropriate opportunity. Most skills are by definition useful, and make a valuable contribution to the well-being of others. While I'm being skilful, I'm in charge, mistress or master of my world. Beyond competence, the performance of a skill has a beauty of its own. The control, timing and confidence of skilful people, for example in sport or performance art, can often transcend even 'top class' criteria to have the same effect upon us as great music, painting or poetry, touching us in that special way which marks the mystical or spiritual experience.

All skills can be practised at the level of art, as in Pirsig's appreciation of the welder, where the striving disappears and the performance looks effortless. If lucky enough to be performing at this level, it feels as if 'we can't put a foot wrong'. Here there is a sense of participation in something which is larger than any one individual life. The skilled person as artist serves their material, allowing it to pass through them, their long technical practice a necessary but insufficient component of the performance.

While many people experience this feeling of mastery at some time in their lives, it is not an everyday occurence. Most of the time this level of performance is not necessary or possible, and yet we still describe a person as skilful. So there are different degrees or levels of skill which in the heyday of the craftsmanship were formally recognized as ranks or statuses. You began as an apprentice, served your time and passed out to be a journeyman. Some people went on to become master craftsmen, and a very few attained the status of artists. These ranks parallel our stages or modes of managing described in Chapter 3.

The *apprentice* is learning rules, procedures and standard ways of doing things. The apprentice tries to do the 'right' thing, copies elders and betters, and spends most of the time practising (Stage /Mode 1).

The *journeyman* operates to the norms and conventions of the trade and can do most jobs in accordance with current standards (Stage/Mode 2). The *master* is beyond simple competence and is able to apply skill in new and complex situations. Flexibility and creativity are important; the master tackles the non-standard jobs (Stage/Mode 3). The *artist* is a master craftsperson operating with a wider awareness in diverse and trackless conditions with a clear sense of purpose. Able to contribute to the particular needs of the time, the artist uses the skills of the trade to serve a higher purpose (Stages/Modes 4 and 5).

However, this is not a simple hierarchy of skill, because whilst few people will attain 'world class' status in any skill, everyone can strive for and achieve artistic levels in what they do. Intention and purpose come into it as well as skill - for example, I'm quite happy as a journeyman gardener and an apprentice poultry-keeper, but I've mastered cooking and on occasions can achieve truly artistic effects. I have many basic abilities but I try harder at cooking, get feedback from (usually) appreciative consumers and derive much satisfaction from it. In my house I'm quite a famous cook - one of the most famous, in fact. Doing a job that needs doing, having a chance to practise my art; all this and fame too - what more can I ask from life? (Well, quite a lot, actually, but it's a start.)

HOW SKILFUL ARE YOU?

What about your skills? Why have you learned some skills and not others? Why have you continued learning in some and put others on automatic? Table 5.1 lists a selection of domestic skills together with a grading system across the top to check whether you have the skill at all and, if so, at what level.

There will be many reasons why you have or have not learned some of these skills. The first column in the table will be one of the most interesting. What is the pattern it reveals in terms of what you can and can't do? And what does this say about you and your attitude to these skills?

Much formal management training is criticized as being too

Skill	Level of skill				
	Can't /Don't do	Apprentice	Competent worker	Craftsman /woman	Artist
1. Cooking					
2. Painting & decorating					
3. Woodwork					
4. Sewing					
5. Knitting					
6. Gardening					
7. Playing a musical instrument					
8. Handwriting					
9. Electrical work					
10. Clothes making					
11. Driving					
12. Car maintenance					
13. Keyboard skills					
14. Operating video equipment					
15. Plumbing					
16. Household budgeting					
17. Ironing					
18. Others					

concerned with teaching techniques for problem-solving, decision-making, time-management, selling and so on as if everyone had the same problems or were not practising these skills because they don't know how to. Because skills are personal qualities and there are uniquely personal patterns in their development, the skills a person has learned so far in life to some extent determine what new skills will be learned in future.

To take an example, if I've never learned keyboard skills because I see myself as not very dexterous, or because I'm 'useless with machines' or because I expect others to do the menial work, then I'm less likely to want to tackle the operation of a PC or any sort of office machine. On the other hand, if I'm good with machines or 'handy' then I might well pick up these skills in preference to others, say, involving communicating with other people.

Looking down your left-hand column, consider some possible reasons why you've not learned some of these basic life skills. How is it that you can't sew or drive a car at your age? The decisions that determine this were probably made somewhere between birth and adulthood. The young child wants to learn everything and will tackle all new skills - crawling, walking, talking, reading - unless discouraged. Adolescents start deciding for themselves *not* to learn certain skills, and also, perhaps, to concentrate upon others. Can you get your kids to help in the garden? Cook? Paint the front door? Perhaps they will learn some of these things later, perhaps not. This early development has all sorts of implications for how we will tackle the skills of managing ourselves and others later in life.

As we saw in Chapter 4, what we manage to do or stop ourselves doing depends upon how we see ourselves, and, in general what stops us tackling things is a fear of failure. Sisters or brothers might avoid or respond to rivalry, determined not to learn to knit because 'she does it', or wanting to learn to paint because 'big brother does it'. Patterns of learning usually involve being independent of or dependent on others. Learning to drive, cook, budget helps with independence, but why do we *not* learn those other useful skills? Could it be that we still expect parents (or parental replacements) to do these things for us? What are your dependency patterns? Whatever patterns you have acquired from home will also apply somehow in the job you do and how you manage.

There are other patterns too which may be reflected in other columns of the table. Are you a multi-skilled person or a specialist? Are you one of life's craftsmen or craftswomen in everything you do, or do you have a wide range of skill levels - an apprentice in this, an artist in that? Do you settle for competence in all things, never letting your reach exceed your grasp, or do you strive continuously for perfection, artistry (even in sweeping the hall)? Can you see a mirror of these patterns in your more complex social and managing skills?

THE SKILLS OF MANAGING

There are three broad groups of useful skills:

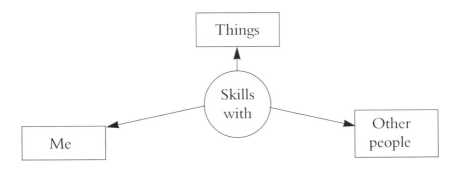

Fig 5.1 : The Skills of Managing

There are many quite complex *things* in managing in which most managers need at least some competence - plans, accounts, budgets, forecasts, policies and so on. Your patterns and preferences revealed by Table 5.1 apply as much to these as much as they do to basic life skills. Skills with *me* - managing yourself - are the main focus of this book. Chapters 2, 3, and 4 are aimed at helping you become more aware of your strengths and weaknesses and how you can manage yourself with regard to these, but there are also some practical skills with yourself such as managing your time, diary management, developing good working habits and so on. Much management training and development concentrates upon these rational, practical skills, so there should be plenty of resources around should you wish to pursue these. The third group of skills - those with *other people* - are particularly crucial to good managing.

Activity 9 on p.190 provides a method for evaluating your skills in this area.

You will have had some of the skills set out in Activity 9 from a very early age, possessing natural ability perhaps, and probably as a result of conditioning from your parents and others. Were you told, 'Children should be seen but not heard' or were you encouraged to join in? To what extent were you encouraged to say, 'Yes' or 'No'? If you were encouraged to be forward, to fend for yourself and to take initiatives with other people, you will find this easier in managing than if you were not. Sometimes early conditioning encourages us to develop certain skills and sometimes quite the opposite. Some people develop strong skills of resistance and opposition to this sort of pressure, and that will certainly become apparent at work. Even if you did the contrary to what your teachers and parents wanted, then you are just as much formed by that.

It is important to understand these patterns of skill learning because unless you understand these early influences and patterns, you may try to work against rather than with them. The starting point then is, what skills with *yourself*, with *things* and with *other people* do you want to develop? And what do you *not* want to work on?

DEVELOPING A SKILL

What is involved in developing a skill? Before looking at the seven elements explained below, it is worthwhile reflecting on a skill you've learned at some point in the past.

Activity 10 on p.192 helps to do this. Working through your own personal case example in this Activity will demonstrate the characteristics of the skills development process.

People learn things in different ways, but the process will usually involve these seven elements:

1. choosing the skill to be learned

2. setting a target to aim at

3. finding a model or models to imitate

4. observing the skilled performance of your model(s)

5. having opportunities to practise

6. obtaining feedback on your performance

7. being supported in learning.

Because skill development takes time and persistence, this last one is more important than we might at first think. For any adult or manager it demands courage simply to start by acknowledging the need for learning - after all, we are supposed to be self-sufficient and grown up - so support is helpful simply to believe that learning new skills is a healthy, natural process of renewal.

Getting started on learning a new skill involves choosing and making a personal commitment of time and attention. All people learn from modelling - sitting next to Nelly or Norman and watching them work. How much of your managing have you learned this way? Yet although much can be learned from others, plenty of practice and feedback is needed to help us learn our own way of doing things. In fact, the feedback and support needed, especially to keep going on the flat bits of the learning curve, illustrate again how important other people are in managing yourself.

This is a central paradox of self-management - as soon as you take personal responsibility for your health, skills and so on, it becomes obvious how much you rely upon the ideas, feedback resources and support of others. Chapter 7 offers various ideas for enlisting the help and support of other people in your self-managing efforts.

The following exercise sets out a process for developing skills. To begin, think of a skill which you would like to learn, either from scratch or to a higher degree of proficiency which is relevant to managing yourself or other people. Select one you really do want to learn, but never had the time, or one that you started on, perhaps many years ago, and that you would now like to take further.

Exercise

- First *visualize* what it would be like to have this skill. What would you be doing with it? Where would you be doing it? Who with? How would you feel being able to do this skill?

- Next, think about your *motivation* to learn this skill. How strong is this? What level of effort will it support? How can you build up your commitment?

- Next, given your level of motivation, what would be a realistic *target* to attain by the end of this week? By the end of this month? In three months' time? Visualize these targets - get a picture of what you could do at these times. Set a series of realistic goals.

- Next, how much practice will be necessary for you to achieve these targets? How much time and opportunity have you for this? Make out a practice timetable and book these practice slots in your diary.

- Who do you know who could be a *model* for you?

- Ask your model(s) for *feedback*. Ask them if they are willing to act as your coach in developing this skill. Whatever skill you're practising, observers who will give you immediate feedback are vital. You can review your practice, going through what happened step by step and looking for improvements you can make, but this is much easier with another person.

- what sources of *support can* you draw on? Who will encourage you, nag you to practise, remind you of your resolve, think about you and talk to you? Will your model or coach do this or do you need to recruit a 'speaking partner' or network of support as well?

MASTERY TO MYSTERY

Skill development can be managed by visualizing the process, investing time in planning, practising and so on, but the last great threshold lies beyond 'mastery'. When we think of ourselves learning a skill, we see ourselves as becoming more and more competent, our control and timing better and better. Yet for many of the skills involved in managing yourself and others the notion of perfect competence is illusory. Those who deal with us in a 'practised' way, the doctor's 'bedside manner', the teacher's elegant explanation, attract both our admiration and irritation. Reassured by professionalism there is a point where we feel patronized by what is ultimately stereotypical treatment. I am not a thing to be worked on to perfection!

Contrarily people demand both competence and professionalism *together with* spontaneity and creativity in human interaction. This means that everyone is bound to get it wrong sometimes; examples of infallibility in human affairs have yet to be discovered. If people describes themselves as 'perfect' at managing we would be entitled to think them, if not deranged, then certainly as appallingly complacent. So here is another paradox: the progression from learner to competent worker to craftsperson to artist is not a gradient of gradually increasing competence, edging step by step to perfection. There is a threshold where mastery gives way to mystery and the creativity of the artist demands the need to get it wrong and to strive against impossible standards.

Because the standards of artistry are not attainable on a regular basis, beyond a certain level of competence it becomes clear that we must admit to ourselves the mysteriousness of things, of the fullness and infinite variety of things. Going beyond competence requires what Rudolf Steiner has described as 'super senses' beyond the five senses of touch, taste, hearing, smell and sight. As our senses provide the data from which we learn and develop, this is an intriguing proposal.

Everyone has experienced occasions when they somehow just know what to say, or what to do. This is sometimes called a 'sixth sense' or 'just common sense'. Yet this is anything but 'common'. The term is used in the absence of understanding how or why we did what we did. We behaved very skilfully but we don't know quite how. The process is somewhat mysterious.

THE SUPER SENSES

Figure 5.2 puts me at the centre, developing most of my skills with myself, with things and with other people through the medium of the normal five senses. Artistry requires us to be in touch with the twelve super senses that lie beyond:

The twelve super senses are:

Sense of life
Awareness of your state of well-being, physical self, aliveness, mood, and so on. 'How are you feeling today?' we ask. This sense of life enables you to take into account the effect of your mood upon others and theirs upon you.

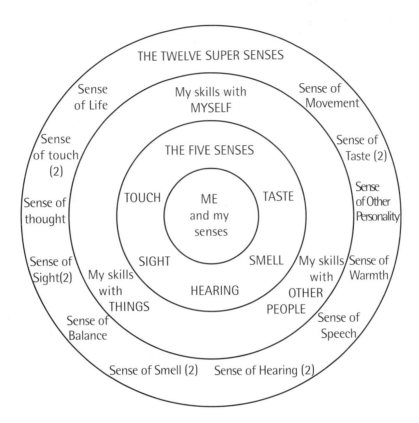

Fig 5.2 : The twelve super senses

Sense of movement
At the physical level this tells you whether you're moving or standing still, and makes you aware of the relative movements of parts of your body. It is this sense that enables you to touch the end of your nose with your eyes shut and at a deeper level which tells you when it's time to make a move, to do or to say something. We say, 'I felt moved to ... (action).'

Sense of balance
At the physical level it's what enables you to stand up without falling over. At a deeper level, we describe ourselves or others as well-balanced, grounded or steady - or as unbalanced or knocked off balance.

Sense of warmth

We experience others as warm or cold and we can sense when we are getting warm - getting to the heart of things.

Sense of speech

When listening we hear more than just what a person says - we say, 'I'm getting the sense of what you're saying', an understanding of what the other person is thinking, feeling and willing.

Sense of thought

As when we say, without the other person speaking, 'I know what you're thinking.' The fully developed sense of thought would be telepathy.

Sense of other personality

Although first impressions can be wrong, we often get a sense, within a few minutes of meeting, of what makes another person as they are. A blind French Resistance leader in the Second World War developed this 'super' sense of personality to such a degree that he was able to judge whether or not candidates who presented themselves for the Resistance could be trusted or not. All those he rejected turned out to be spies. On one occasion his colleagues overruled him because the candidate had such good credentials. A few days later this man, whom the blind leader had correctly sensed to be a danger, betrayed them.

The other five super senses are the transformed versions of the normal five senses:

Sense of sight

A sense of vision or foresight as in 'I see what you mean' or 'I can see difficulties ahead'. Sometimes we may refer to 'second sight' in those who can foresee coming events.

Sense of touch

Being in touch with the situation and with other people; having a feel for what's happening or what someone is doing.

Sense of hearing

When we talk of things resonating within us, as in 'that rings a bell' or 'that person is giving off strong vibrations'.

Sense of taste

When we notice a pleasant or unpleasant taste to something, 'That leaves a nasty taste in the mouth' or 'This is just to my taste'.

Sense of smell

We sniff out situations, perhaps smell 'a rat' or feel that 'something smells fishy' or detect 'a whiff of conspiracy in the air'.

Steiner's twelve super senses are a way of working with the mysterious to become more intuitive and to convert craft into art. Regularly carrying out activities such as the backwards review and 'being aware of what's going on inside you' - your own thinking, feeling, willing (both Chapter 2) - can help develop these 'sixth' senses. Creative visualization, making affirmations, creating silence and space for listening to your inner self through meditating (Chapter 6), can also contribute to what is sometimes described as opening the 'third eye' or of the 'inner sense organs'.

Perhaps you are finding this discussion far-fetched or at least somewhat strange? Well, yes, it is strange, but how would you expect the mysterious to be? These senses are not normal in that they remain largely hidden to those who live just in the world of the five senses. It may be that people who have lost one or more of these 'normal' senses are more likely to have developed some of the super senses - as in the blind French Resistance leader - or that people not seen as normal but as strange or even 'mad' have also developed them. Yet some of these ideas have become more understood and used, for example in medicine where meditation and creative visualization can help people in their struggles with cancer and other diseases. Whether you wish to go beyond mastery in managing yourself and explore in these mysterious depths is, of course, up to you.

6 Managing Your Health

A 36-year-old managing director of a supermarket chain was found dead in his car. He had driven out into the country and connected a tube from the exhaust pipe into the car. Later it was found that he had been sacked from his job just ten hours previously. His former Chairman was quoted as saying three things, 'We are deeply shocked…' 'Although he was very competent at sales and marketing, he unfortunately neglected the day-to-day running of the company… and 'He was an extremely tough character and he took the news like a man.'

This true story is a horrific example of some of the worst possible effects of managerial work. A highly successful young man, making an important contribution in a top job, is suddenly and brutally removed from office. Acknowledged to be good at some things, he is judged to be bad at others. He takes the news 'like a man' and preserves his tough image, but at a cost which turns out to be insupportable.

HOW ARE YOU MANAGING YOUR HEALTH?

Fortunately, such incidents are rare. Yet the working lives of managers and professionals are often demanding and pressurized as well as sedentary. People work long hours that spill over into weekends and evenings; pursue careers single-mindedly, uprooting families frequently to climb the ladder; commute long distances and endure tiring business trips; are responsible for others in circumstances where expediency and moral values clash; pressure themselves with demands for greater excellence or higher achievement and often drink and eat too much as part of this territory.

Work under pressure, especially from chairs behind desks, creates stress. Stress results in a number of physiological responses in human beings, for example:

- increased rate of breathing

- increased production of adrenalin and other hormones

- increased secretion of cholesterol in the liver

- constriction of blood vessels in key muscle areas

- faster heart beat to increase blood supply.

All of these help to prepare us for action, particularly physical action. Triggered by the autonomous nervous system, these instinctive responses probably helped us survive the Stone Age. Our prehistoric forebears needed these instinctive physical changes and responses to cope with predators and used this physical arousedness in real flight or fight. The monsters met in managerial work look a bit different - frustrating meetings, people who let you down, unfair criticisms, failure to meet targets and deadlines, having to do things you don't like or approve of. Nonetheless, monsters they are, and instinctively, if not consciously, your body recognizes this.

How do you cope with these monsters? Are you easily irritated and frustrated? Do you feel intolerant a lot of the time? Or are you mostly quite relaxed at work, easy-going, taking it all in your stride?

To check your behaviour at work and find out whether you are a Type A or Type B personality turn to Activity 11 on p. 193. Then read on, below, to find out the implications of your score.

ACTIVITY 11 Page 193

Activity 11 is based on work done on occupational stress which suggests a link between personality and the tendency to get highly stressed or not. Two heart specialists, Friedman and Rosenman, propose a relationship between coronary heart disease and certain types of behaviour. Their *Type A person* exhibits the following:

- extreme competitiveness

- continuous striving for achievement

- aggressiveness

- impatience and restlessness

- hyper-alertness

- explosiveness of speech

- tenseness of facial musculature

- feelings of being under pressure all the time

- a chronic sense of urgency, of struggle.

On the other hand, their *Type B person* exhibits:

- little sense of time urgency

- little 'free-floating aggression'

- little need to discuss or display achievements

- ability to relax and play without guilt

- slower and more easy-going movements and speech

- feelings which are less easily irritated, frustrated and angered.

The theory is that Type A people suffer more heart disease – between two and six times as much, depending upon the study. There are two other important things to say before interpreting your score: first, Friedman and Rosenman's Types A and B are ideal types, that is to say, not real examples of people but composites of behaviour traits constructed to fit a theory. No individual exactly fits A or B. The second reason is to do with the nature of managerial work. A true Type B might have trouble managing at all with their lack of urgency and low need for achievement. Movers and shakers, the people who fix things and get things done, surely tend towards Type A.

But if managers, as Type As, enjoy influencing their environment and making things happen, this can bring associated problems. Type As frequently overdo it – driving as if their lives depended upon shaving two seconds off the journey time; being unable to wait patiently in the shortest queues; using high energy on trivial tasks. Addicted to adrenalin, they are a pain to those around them – always pushing, aggressive, unsettling, never still – and ultimately perhaps a pain to themselves. If you have noticed yourself getting a little irritated or impatient by the gap between the quiz and the scoring key below, is that a Type A indicator?

If your score for Activity 11 was:

- between 8 and 15 – you are Type B

- between 16 and 23 – you lean towards Type B

- exactly 24 – Congratulations! (or Cheat!)

- between 25 and 32 – you lean towards Type A

- between 33 and 40 – you are Type A Plus.

If you lean towards Type B, your needs as a person and manager may be more to do with other chapters in this book, especially those on skills and action. If you tend towards Type A then this chapter could be most important for you. The characteristics which are serving you well in your managerial career may also be having some undesirable consequences. To manage yourself, you need to be aware of all aspects of your health - monitoring it, diagnosing it from time to time and acting on it regularly.

One of the main problems is that people become physiologically aroused by the stress factors at work, creating a readiness for fight or flight but, unlike our Stone Age ancestors, with no appropriate physical action for expressing it. Being subject to these stress factors over long periods without appropriate release and expression is damaging to health. The main killers of managers and professional workers are heart disease (easily the biggest), cancer and strokes. The link between stress and heart disease and strokes is well established, and it is now becoming clear that a number of forms of cancer are related to the way we handle our emotions - to say nothing of those that are self-induced by smoking.

The good news is that the risk of many of these diseases can be reduced by developing healthy habits. Good health is not just about avoiding an early grave. Many stress-related illnesses are not killers - arthritis, asthma, ulcers, colitis, diabetes, eczema and migraines are just a few from a long and unpleasant list. Some of these illnesses may be psychosomatic - physical manifestations of psychological disturbances - and good health also means freedom from, or control over, emotional ills such as anxiety, fear, panic, anger, hatred, resentment and guilt, feelings of helplessness and inadequacy. Mental distress such as hypertension, neurosis, manic depression, obsession, phobias and hysteria can be as crippling as any physical illness.

Dividing these dangers to health into physical, emotional and mental is rather simplistic - illnesses affect whole persons - body, soul and spirit - but it has the benefit of illustrating what you can do to guard against these dangers.

Before looking at these three aspects of health, first examine your own attitudes to your health by working through Activity 12 on p.194.

Destructive habits - such as smoking, too much drinking and eating - develop for all sorts of reasons, from parents, adolescent role models, at times of stress and so on, and as they become habitual we are no longer aware of them or their effects. Some are a product of the rich world lifestyle where the high material standard of living provides an abundance of food, alcohol, cigarettes, drugs, cars, and so on. Heart disease, alcoholism, lung cancer, diabetes and obesity are diseases of affluence. In poor countries peoples are largely free from these diseases, suffering instead from lack of food, clean water, adequate housing and sanitation - and the consequent diseases of poverty.

Managing your health is a critical aspect of 'self-development'. Eating too much at business lunches or bottling up feelings for fear of appearing weak is harmful and sets a bad example to others. It's bad for you, bad for them, bad for business.

So what can be done? Talk is cheap, and habits are hard to break. First, become aware of what you are doing. Not noticing, blocking awareness of unpleasant facts, not remembering and so on are common self-protective devices - yet in these circumstances they add to the self-harm by allowing it to continue. This is our inner enemy (Chapter 4) suppressing the truth, yet another part of us - the higher self - knows how bad these habits are and provides a way out. Simple awareness, receptivity to what is happening is not easy and can be painful, but it is the key to tackling these habits and replacing them with healthy ones. A part of you - your inner friend - has always to remain on watch when you're in the pub, the restaurant, the office. Awareness and vigilance are the main actions required for the tough and lonely work of habit-breaking.

Enlisting the support of others is the second key step to healthy habits. The support of sympathetic allies is important especially because if people aren't with you then they may be against you. Those who press upon others extra drinks and 'just one' cigarette are looking for allies too. The managerial work environment seems to produce many such 'friends', and if you want to break your self-destructive habits and build new, healthy ones, then a support group or self-development group (Chapter 7) could be part of the answer.

Work as art and addiction

Sometimes stress and stress-related illness is presented as just a managerial or executive problem, but this is not the case at all. Manual, clerical and technical workers are just as likely to suffer from stress, and much more so from poor conditions, monotonous work, overloading, tight targets, high quality standards and heavy supervision. Managers generally have more discretion and more control over their working lives - which creates both the opportunities for the initiative and risk-taking that many thrive upon *and* the stress caused by overloading.

In discussing health we may tend to dwell too much on the debilitating effects of work, under-emphasizing its excitement and fulfilling nature. Much of our lives is spent working and work provides so much, including money, social standing, status, identity and a time structure, by the day, week, year, even for life. Social lives often centre round work. And work can also offer the precious opportunity of feeling competent in exercising skills and abilities in a collaborative production that is of use to others.

With all this and money too, it is no wonder that we can be in danger of addiction, of 'workaholism'. Many people get a real 'kick' out of their work, but when this becomes compulsive, taking over lives, blotting out family, leisure, friends, let alone politics, world affairs, music, art, games and all the other available riches, there is a problem. Over-dependent upon work, eventually retirement or redundancy loom ahead like wastelands - we try not to think of them.

'Great work', it has to be said, is often bad for your health. Many great artists die young. If the exhaustion of producing great efforts doesn't kill you, then the frustration caused by the inability to attain your vision may drive you to drink. There are choices to make here. Should Franz Schubert have gone a little easier on himself, maybe even finishing off his symphony and living to a ripe old age, instead of producing, in a short but phenomenally energetic burst, over six hundred incomparable songs and dying at thirty-one with a solid place in the history books?

Work can be all. In his book, *Learning in Organisations* (Open University Press, 1993), David Casey speaks of the many chief executives with whom he has worked, and is struck by how much such people have sacrificed to their single-minded careers and how many of them are now lonely and isolated people. Is this sacrifice upon the altar of great managerial art worth it for you? Whatever your answer to this conundrum, the lessons of managing yourself first, looking after yourself, and caring for yourself, still apply.

ATTITUDES FOR GOOD HEALTH

What does the word 'fitness' mean to you? Do you think of an athlete or some other supremely physically fit character? In Chapter 1, we suggested that being fit means being ready or suited for something. Are you fit to be a manager? Can you fit this role? Fitness in this sense is attaining and maintaining a state of readiness for action and it involves all aspects of ourselves; we need physical, emotional and mental fitness.

A good manager needs a certain level of physical fitness, but also to be fit in terms of social skills (including, communication, assertiveness, negotiation); mental skills (including, awareness, sensitivity to events, ability to make judgements); and especially in terms of the ability to act (including, initiating, risk-taking, using physical, emotional and mental energy). No one can stay fit in all these ways without managing themselves first. If you don't make it a priority, you don't keep fit. Here are five key attitudes which are essential to good health.

Believing in the possibility of illness.

Amazing though it may be many people refuse to believe in the possibility of ill health. People frequently deny that there is anything wrong with them; symptoms are suppressed, medical check-ups are resisted and doctors are avoided. Either out of fear or a 'grin and bear it' attitude, this is a block to managing your health. A simple acknowledgement of the possibility of being ill is an important first step.

Believing that you have some control over your own health

Those who deny that they could ever be ill often also think that their health is entirely outside their control. This is a sort of fatalism - 'if the bullet has my name on it, then it's no good worrying' - and is a foolish attitude because, although we can't change our genetic inheritance or prevent 'acts of God', how we live our lives affects our health a great deal. Much of this is under our control.

Recognizing self-destructive habits when you see them

As already noted, people can blank out their awareness of what they're doing and 'know' is bad for them. Can you bear to look at what you are doing to yourself?

Being able to give yourself treats

Self-destructive habits are hard to give up, 'It's the only pleasure I have left,' we say, forcing down another helping. Being able to treat yourself and being able to recognize when you need a treat is important. Some men seem to be particularly bad at this. 'Real men' ought to be able to take the heat in the kitchen without pampering themselves with hot baths, taking half days off, wearing favourite clothes or taking a break with a good book for half an hour. Yet these sorts of treats are an essential part of breaking self-destructive habits and making sure you stay fit and healthy.

Feeling able to look after yourself

This means having the knowledge and giving yourself the 'permission' to look after yourself. People can often stop themselves doing helpful things - like not giving themselves permission to relax, take time off, or whatever.

Having looked at your attitudes to health, we can now go on to some ideas for looking after yourself and managing your health.

LOOKING AFTER YOURSELF

This section includes only a small sample of what is available in terms of activities and exercises to help you manage your health, but there are plenty of other good books on this aspect of managing yourself.

Two everyday sayings sum up the basics of managing your health. When we say to friends or relations, 'Now, do look after yourself' - meaning eat regular meals, get plenty of sleep, keep warm and so on - we recognize these things as important for basic survival and maintenance. Then we sometimes say, 'I'm keeping fit' or 'getting fit' - building up muscles, losing weight, building physical endurance, speed or flexibility - through exercise. Looking after yourself and getting fit are both developmental activities - they imply a getting or staying fit *for* something, a next step.

The old ideal of 'a sound mind in a sound body' means emotional and mental as well as physical health, but emotional and mental fitness may be less easy to consider for some people. Some of those key attitudes are especially powerfully here; to accept that things can be done to prevent or cure mental or emotional ill health we must first accept its possibility. Because stress in managerial work is more or less endemic, you need to keep fit for the emotional and mental pressures of your work.

We start below with physical exercises - which help keep your mind as well as your body healthy (these parts not being as separate as everyday speech implies) - before going on to some activities to help with mental and emotional fitness.

Climbing exercise

Climb 50 steps a day. That's it! Do it as slowly or as quickly as you like - as long as it makes you blow a bit to exercise the heart and lungs. Learn to check your pulse, normally about 60-70, and push it up a bit - but if you start to get dizzy or feel pain, slow down. As a rule of thumb your pulse rate should never exceed 220 minus your age.

Do this every day and it will help protect you from heart disease. Tests on American managers showed that just climbing fifty steps a day significantly lowered their susceptibility to heart disease. If you don't manage anything else in this book, do this; you will have had your money's worth and more.

The great thing about physical exercise is that it makes you feel better - not just physically, but emotionally and mentally too. Try it. Feel like strangling the cat? Run up and down fifty stairs. Feel depressed and low? Run up and down fifty stairs. This is easier and less obtrusive than jogging - you can do it anywhere, on business or on holiday - and no one need even know what you're up to!

Good health requires exercise. And it is surprising how much even a little helps. The important thing is to do it by habit - every day. Here's another simple one - bending and stretching - which anyone can do at their own speed and level of effort. Try to achieve a daily discipline, even with a shortened or token version of your normal routine.

Bending and stretching exercise

This improves suppleness and flexibility and may therefore cause some pain - again, don't overdo it. Wear loose clothing.

- *Step 1* Stand, feet a foot or so apart, and attempt to touch your toes. Repeat three, five or ten times. It doesn't matter whether you can touch them or not - just push to feel that stretching of the lower back and the back of the knees. You can intersperse Step 1 with Step 2.

- *Step 2* Stand, reach for the sky, stretching upwards, hands above your head, rising on to tip-toe. Hold for five seconds. Repeat as Step 1. You should feel the stretching in arms, legs, neck and back. Deliberately stretch each bit of you from toes to legs to back to neck to arms to fingers.

- *Step 3* This is a twister. Stand, feet eighteen inches apart, hold both arms out straight in front, palms down. Now swing both arms round to the right as far as you can go, maintaining the position of arms (and legs). The right arm will reach much farther than the left pointing behind you. Now swing right round, still holding the arms in position, to the left. Repeat five or ten times each side.

- *Step 4* One for the neck - a key tension point. Kneel and sit on your heels, fold your arms behind your back and rotate your head clockwise, stretching your neck as much as possible. Then rotate anti-clockwise. Repeat three or five times. Bend your head down (so you can see your chest), up (so you can see the ceiling), and as far as possible to either side.

- *Step 5* One for the stomach. Lie on your back on the floor. Use a book or towel to make your head comfortable. Raise your right leg, holding it straight, as far as you can. Lower it and repeat with the left leg. Repeat three, five or ten times. You can make this more strenuous by turning it into trunk curls: hook your feet under the bed or other low bar, put your hands behind your head and curl up as far as you can, keeping your legs straight.

These exercises are not meant to be strenuous, but rather to be an enjoyable and meditative routine that you can make into a habit. We don't want to add to the distaste which many people still have due to forced activities at school. Take care that the competitiveness that abounds in the management environment does not spill over and turn your physical exercises into Olympian efforts. This is not a competition so the rules and the learning required are quite different.

Obviously, if you want something more demanding in the way of physical exercise, there are plenty of books available. The next exercise is a physical one too, but this time it is about relaxing, with quite a different feel from the first two.

Relaxation exercise

- *Step 1* Find a quiet place where you can sit comfortably but upright, both feet on the ground, head up, back straight. Some people do this cross-legged, or even lying down as in Step 5 of Bending and Stretching, but you may be more comfortable in a chair.

- *Step 2* When comfortable, close your eyes and consciously relax all your muscles, starting at the top of your head, down through your forehead, ears mouth, jaw, neck, shoulders and so on, going very slowly and becoming conscious of each muscle group as you go. Go right down to your toes.

Try to get into each group of muscles - *be* your neck, totally absorbed there before moving on. You can imagine that you're going deeper ... and deeper ... sinking down in warm water, or in a lift, or to the bottom of the sea. Take your time.

- *Step 3* Begin to breathe in deeply through your nose and then out through your mouth. Listen to your breath come in ... and go out .... Notice that there is a pause as you finish breathing out ... and before you begin to breathe in.

As you relax, you will find your breathing becoming shallower. Become very aware of your breathing and nothing else ... notice as it becomes slower, more restful.

- *Step 4* Continue breathing but begin to count backwards from ten to one in the pauses. So, breathe out - ten; breathe in - nine; breathe out - eight; breath in - seven ... and so on down to one, then back up to ten, down to one again and so on.

You can carry on like this for five, ten or even twenty minutes, concentrating wholly on your breathing. You may have stray thoughts but don't worry about them, just let them come and go.

As with most exercise, you get better at relaxation with practice. With practice, you can develop what has been called the 'relaxation response' and be able to call upon it even in stressful situations. This is an excellent survival tool that should be in every manager's briefcase.

The relaxation response is like meditation in some ways - a daily discipline that improves with practice. Meditation is the traditional Eastern route to self-knowledge and self-development and is a good way to reduce anxiety and tension, to improve clear thinking and relaxation. Many meditations involve the contemplation of objects, which is easier than thinking about words or ideas. Here is one meditation out of the many. Again, you need a quiet place in which to sit or lie down comfortably.

Meditation exercise

- *Step 1* Choose a flower and place it in front of you. (Pick another object if you wish - a piece of jewellery, pottery or wood. The flower has the advantage of being alive so the rest of this exercise is based upon this.)

- *Step 2* Note carefully all the characteristics of the flower: its colour, the shape of its petals, the markings, the texture. Take your time. Study each aspect in turn, dwell upon it.

- *Step 3* Think back from the flower to its beginnings as a seed. Think about the seed in the soil beginning to grow. Imagine the life forces in the seed, now asleep, now beginning to stir and awake. Imagine the seed shooting, pushing up from the earth, reaching for the light. Imagine the roots growing downwards into the earth seeking water and nutriments from the soil.

- *Step 4* Now see the shoot breaking into the air, opening out, receiving warmth and light from the sun, water from the dew and rain. See the buds developing and beginning to open out. Soon you have the flower you see before you.

- *Step 5* Think on from the flower as it is. Imagine it

> reaching its peak of maturity and beginning to die down. Imagine the seeds being produced. See them fall to earth with the petals. Now you are at the end and the beginning of the flower.
>
> As you go through the stages, see if you can imagine what it feels like to be that seed, that shoot, those roots, that flower. Feel, in Dylan Thomas' words, 'the force that through the green fuse drives the flower' as this life force is born, grows to maturity and dies away again.

As we have moved from physical exercises to relaxation and meditation, it may have become clearer how body and mind, physical and mental/emotional states are not separate at all but closely interlinked. Maintaining and developing a healthy body also contributes to creating a healthy mind.

DEVELOPING A HEALTHY MIND

A healthy mind is free from chronic phobias and constant euphoria. It is healthy to feel joy on a sunny day, fear and anxiety when you're in a difficult spot, or grief when someone you love leaves you, but these feelings are normally transient, giving way to memory and equanimity as the events become part of us, part of our biographies. A healthy mind maintains emotional balance; being aware of feelings but not overwhelmed by them. A fear of being overwhelmed by feelings to the point of being unable to function may lead to denial or repression of emotions. The professional exercising skill without compassion is as out of balance as the person disabled from acting by strong and uncontrolled emotions. A healthy mind is above all a balanced one. Healthy people have 'their feet on the ground'; to be unbalanced is to be ill.

A sound or balanced mind is neither dogmatic nor full of its own ideas nor over-reliant upon the ideas of others. If you can listen to others, respect their views and yet disagree with them when you wish on the basis of your own clear and consistent views, then you have a 'balanced view' or an 'open mind'. Take, for example, the balance needed between attention to detail and the ability to see the big picture. A healthy mind can deal with both - grasp the detail of the situation and get an overview of the general principles involved. Getting 'bogged down in trivia' or always generalizing 'with your head in the clouds' are both extreme consequences of 'either... or...' thinking. Neither attitude is healthy. The key to the healthy mind lies not in this or that, but in a balance between two equally desirable and complementary qualities which, if either were to exist alone, would become exaggerated and unhealthy.

To keep your balance as a manager or professional there are also the balances between work and play, home and work, thinking and doing, material rewards and the artistic or spiritual self. Imbalances here lead to excess or impoverishment, cause considerable stress, may contribute to the break-up of families and relationships and eventually the lopsided development of the person. Managing yourself for a healthy mind and a balanced life is the first requirement for managing others in a healthy way.

Take time now to consider how you look after yourself. How do you manage your stress? Before reading on turn now to Activity 13 on p.196.

Some people are good at coping but also very self-critical, finding it difficult to forgive themselves for failures and disappointments. Managers who set themselves high standards can fall into this category. Being able to treat yourself is the necessary balance to setting yourself high standards:

Treats

'Treats' are rewards or gifts you give yourself for hard work or hard times. It is often the little things that give us great pleasure - a walk in the park at lunchtime, an hour with a favourite book, a bath at the end of a hard day.

• *Step 1* Write down all the ways in which you give treats to yourself.

• *Step 2* Look at your week (or day, month) and plan in some treats to reward yourself after tough meetings, hard days, unpleasant tasks, prodigious efforts etc.

• *Step 3* Make this a habit.

Were you stuck for ideas about treats? Why not ask your friends or colleagues what they do. Everyone treats themselves from time to time - although some are much better at it than others! Never mind, you'll get better with practice. Here is a list we shared with each other: having a hot bath; taking two weekdays off a month to go walking; going away for the weekend; doing the newspaper crossword with my partner; buying some flowers; buying chocolate; finding a kitten to stroke; and taking my child to a football match.

Treats are important to all of us, and it is still often men who need to learn how to treat and nurture themselves and others. There is still often a gender gap when it comes to those who do the 'caring work', the 'emotional specialists' who bring up children, look after sick relatives and aged parents, nurture partners after hard days at work. Women may often be better at giving themselves treats and when you're good at giving yourself treats, you are more likely to give others treats too.

Here's another everyday exercise involving talking to yourself. Given some regard for other people's inhibitions, talking to yourself is a healthy thing to do. It helps you not to bottle things up and also to rehearse things before they happen. If there is no one else to help, you can help yourself. You can try out new approaches to problems or deal with any bad feelings that might fester inside you if you don't get them out.

Talking to yourself

Long held to be a sign of madness, this can be a good way of staying sane (though it might be best to avoid doing it out loud in busy offices). Talking to or with yourself can put you in touch with your feelings and that 'inner voice' - or inner friend from Chapter 3. When you are faced, in the absence of a supportive friend, with a difficult problem or a frustrating or hurtful situation, you can counsel yourself.

• *Step 1*   Find a quiet place to be with yourself. This is important even if you are going to talk to yourself silently. It is better to speak to yourself out loud, and one way of doing this is to use a tape recorder. This has the advantage of preserving what you say, but it might make you too self-conscious. You might like to do it while out walking - although you can sometimes get so absorbed in the conversation that you fail to notice fellow walkers, who tend to edge past warily.

• *Step 2*   Tell yourself the story, explain the problem or describe the event.

• *Step 3*   Now talk about the feelings you have about this problem or event.

• *Step 4*   What possible courses of action are there? What are the options and their consequences?

The exercises and activities in this chapter aim to help you manage your health better. Some of them also apply to the other aspects of managing yourself - your skills, action and identity. Equally, some of the exercises in earlier chapters have a bearing upon healthy living, working and managing. In the next chapter we go on to look at the crucial business of managing yourself with other people.

7 Working With Other People

Ironically, it is when we take the personal responsibility for managing ourselves that we need others most. At first sight it looks like you should 'Do-It-Yourself', but when you get down to managing yourself - your survival, maintenance and development - then, standing alone, your resources look rather slim. Relationships are perhaps the major source of development for human beings; we grow in a reciprocal giving to and taking from each other, and few people can sustain the solo self-management effort for very long. Managing yourself requires both the support and the challenge that only other people can give.

Some years ago we went to a large organization to work with the managers on developing themselves. After informal research some 50 managers were given copies of a guide to managers' self-development and invited to use it for their own self-development. On returning to the company two months later we discovered some interesting facts, which could be generalized far beyond this particular sample of managers. Four or five of these managers had made good progress, reporting significant steps forward in knowledge, skills or understanding - one engineer even kept the book by him, to work on in slack moments. On the other hand, at least as many could scarcely remember the book; the great majority claimed to have read all or parts of it, but had done nothing to change the way they managed as a consequence.

On this evidence, a Parkinsonian law can be posited: Any attempt to make available unsupported self-development opportunities will result in ten per cent of people seizing the chance and making good use of it. But 90 per cent will not. Furthermore the active ten per cent are probably the ones who are learning and self-developing anyway; that is, they are the ten per cent least in need of it.

Efforts at self-development and managing yourself are much more likely to succeed with support and comradeship from other resourceful human beings. This chapter is about harnessing and setting up these sources of support and help. Here are four main ways of doing this:

- finding a friend: working with a 'speaking partner'

- finding allies: using your role set

- making contacts: networking

- getting comrades: creating a self-development group.

The first three of these can be done in all organizations, but not all workplaces will support the fourth. However, like the other three it can be done outside any work organization. You only need the cooperation of one other person to have a speaking partner and you can apply the idea of role set and network to any aspect of life. Setting up a self-development group is more demanding but you will find ideas about how to do this later in the chapter. The key point is to ensure that you establish some method(s) of support and help for your self-managing enterprise

WORKING WITH A 'SPEAKING PARTNER': FINDING A FRIEND

A speaking partner is someone you meet from time to time to discuss how you are managing yourself, someone to discuss ideas with, to share good and bad experiences with, someone who will offer feedback, support and challenge. This may be someone at a similar point to you in their own development - a fellow self-developer with whom you have a co-counselling relationship, splitting the time so that each acts as talker and listener in turns. Or it may be an older person prepared to listen, question and offer their experience - more like a mentor.

How do you choose a speaking partner? Your 'best friend' is

probably not a good choice; you may be too close and lack detachment, but most of all this is a different sort of relationship. A good choice would be someone from another department whom you like or have met on a course or in the process of a project. Someone who is also interested in their self-management or perhaps even someone going through a crisis in their biography might be most appropriate. If you want to learn from an older person whose style you admire, they might be prepared to give you an hour or two every month.

The main criterion is that the person should be interested and prepared to work with you over a period of time - at least six months or a year. If you're still stuck, try the networking activity later in this chapter and see whether anyone emerges from this.

Once you have a partner, what do you talk about? Whatever you wish; whatever problem, difficulty, interest or topic is relevant at this point in managing yourself. If you are following the ideas in this book then you will have no shortage of starting points. For example:

- entries in your personal journal or diary

- some action or change in the way you do things which you've been trying

- a critical incident which has just happened - 'the most difficult (managerial) situation I have had to face in the last week/ fortnight/ month'

- something you have read

- something that has been on your mind - a worry, a nagging doubt.

To work well with a speaking partner make sure you arrange the time and place properly. Meeting somewhere for lunch might be a good way to warm up, but it's not the best setting for good talking and listening. Find a suitable place and book it for a suitable time, just like any other appointment or business meeting. This might be a quiet corner with two comfortable chairs, or even a walk round the park where you can achieve the three objectives - of free talk, supportive listening and constructive responding.

Free talk

Readiness is a key principle in managing yourself - being ready and willing - simply feeling free and ready to talk about the issue or topic; free from distractions (telephones, interruptions, general environmental noise); and ready, in the sense of feeling this is the right time to talk about this subject with this person.

Supportive listening

At the heart of a good relationship with a speaking partner lies supportive listening.

Stop reading for a minute and reflect on your own experience. Jot down the names of three or four people who have been helpful to you in the past. Now jot down what it was about each of those people that made them helpful. The chances are that your list reads something like this:

- they were sympathetic and understanding

- they showed interest in what I was saying

- they respected me and my feelings

- they still liked me even when I made mistakes or did stupid things

- they sometimes challenged me and made me think

- they told me how they saw me, but in a way that helped me to listen to them.

You may also have on your list that someone gave you helpful advice. If so, this was probably not of the 'If I were you ...' type of advice. In choosing our own path, judicious advice is often what we seek, but wise people give it very sparingly and accept it very cautiously. As Lao Tse says, 'the one who speaks does not know and the one who knows does not speak'. A good purpose for the speaking partnership is to help us generate our own solutions. As a supportive listener, the main aim is to try and manifest the qualities contained in the list above - to achieve those attitudes and actions which we have recognized as helpful to us.

Constructive responding

The twin to supportive listening is constructive responding, and has itself two aspects. The first of these is listening in silence and responding through silently paying attention. Never underestimate the value of silence in these rushed and hyperactive times; what people often need most is the open space, the pool of silence in which to reflect and be reflective. During such silences we may hear our own inner voice, our own inner helper.

Try this exercise for listening silently and with attention - a surprisingly rare occurrence between people but an easy skill to learn.

Agree a time limit with whoever is going to speak first, say ten minutes. Then show your interest and attention by looking your partner in the face. Keep a steady gaze of attention. Your partner will find it unnecessary to look at you all the time, they may look down, up, out of the window; but you will notice they glance back at you from time to time. When you pay attention, do not speak. You are there to listen. Sit out the pauses, don't fill them. Nod if you must, and grunt if otherwise you would burst; but aim to listen in silence and pay silent attention.

This gives any speaker the unusual opportunity for an uninterrupted pursuit of a topic, a chance to explore a problem. In a surprisingly short piece of uninterrupted time a person can explore their thoughts and feelings and desire for action. Through the agency of a silent listener, who by being there and restraining her or his own desire to talk, a vessel is created in which the speaker can sort out ideas, clarify feelings and recognize wishes. If you listen carefully you may be able to pick out your partner's thinking, feeling and doing.

- *Thinking:* What is being said, the pattern of thoughts; is it logical? Detailed or general? In the past, present or future? Who is being talked about and who is not? What images and metaphors are being used? What assumptions are being made?

- *Feeling:* What is the speaker feeling? Notice the gestures, posture, tone of voice, way of breathing and the expression of the face, eye movement.

- *Willing:* What does the person want to do? What is just a wish and what is a definite intention to act?

Listening in this way may seem a bit unusual at first - because it is unusual. If you persevere and overcome the awkwardness of silences, you will find this an attainable skill, and a very valuable one to acquire.

The other face of constructive responding is to act and intervene in various ways. Given the importance of silence and the danger of advice, you may by now feel you unable to say anything for fear of interfering rather than helping. Yet, of course there are some important and helpful responses to make; Figure 7.1 on p.133 shows a simple sevenfold classification. These helpful responses often involve questions to the speaker - usually of a prompting or 'open-ended' kind which encourage the other to talk or to take up a point as yet unexplored. Examples of these sorts of questions follow on from Figure 7.1.

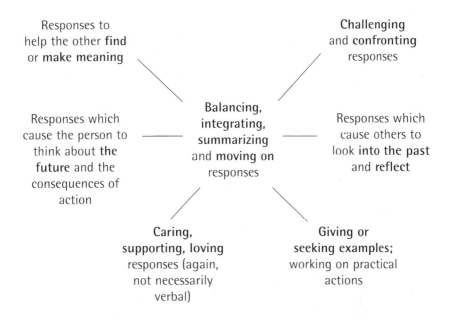

Figure 7.1 : Seven Types of Constructive Responding

Types of constructive responses

1. Caring, supporting, loving responses

- Pay close attention but don't stare. Show that you are listening and hearing with nods and smiles, but don't overdo it.

- Empathize. Say, 'If I were in your place I think I would feel ...' But don't tell the other person what they are feeling (it can sometimes be preferable to say, 'Does that make you feel frightened/happy/jealous etc.?').

- Be warm and encouraging; give the other person positive feedback, e.g., 'I know you are good at ..., I saw you the other day'.

- In some circumstances, you may be able to support the other person by touching them, taking their hand or even giving them a hug. Although touching is taboo for some people, sometimes it is the most helpful thing you can do. On a TV programme concerning children with cancer, an oncologist said that she sometimes just sat and cried with parents. Being with the other person may be the best thing we can do.

2. Challenging and confronting responses

- Point out inconsistencies and contradictions in what your partner is saying, e.g., 'How consistent is what you've just said with the point you made five minutes ago?'

- Look for inconsistencies between words and feelings and actions, for example, 'You say you're not angry but you certainly look it!'

- Say what you feel about what your partner is saying, if possible you can do so straight away and in terms of how you feel about it, for example, 'I don't agree with your view of..., it makes me feel angry.'

- Give negative feedback in as supportive a way as possible, using 'I' statements, e.g., 'I feel attacked by you' rather than, 'You are attacking me'. Remember that most of us can only handle one bit of negative feedback at a time.

3. Responses which help the other find meaning
Ask questions like:
- 'Can you see a pattern in all this, or a theme?'

- 'What is this saying to you?'

- 'Why is this happening to you?'

- 'What does this mean to you?' (But don't put your own meaning on events, and watch out for rationalizations.)

4. Giving examples, practical actions

Ask questions like:

- 'What sort of things are you talking about?'

- 'What type of person do you have difficulty with?'

- 'Can you give examples of other situations in which you feel helpless, angry, upset, etc?'

- 'What's your first step?'

- 'What resources will this require?'

5. Responses which help the other reflect or look into the past

Ask questions like:

- 'Has this happened before?'

- 'What did you do last time?'

- 'Have you felt like this before?'

- 'Give me some examples of incidents like this in the past.' (But don't get trapped in the past or in old guilt and 'if only ...' sentiments.)

6. Responses which cause the other person to think about the future and the consequences of action

Ask questions like:

- 'What do you want to do about this?'

- 'What will be the consequences for yourself and all the others involved?'

- 'What alternatives and options do you have?'

- 'What blocks and obstacles are there?'

- 'Where do you want to be with regard to this in two weeks/six months/a year's time?' (But watch for escapism into the future to avoid the present. Emphasize what can be done now, and move to questions about practical action).

7. Balancing, integrating, summarizing and moving on responses

- Watch the balance of the whole conversation with regard to analysis and action, past and present, thoughts and feelings, and try to integrate them all.

- Be aware of your own thoughts, feelings and wishes - listen to yourself as the listener - and try to remain detached and not allow these to influence what you are hearing from your partner. In particular, is what you are doing/saying in any way being influenced by things you want from the other person?

- Summarize what your partner has said in order to get confirmation of points or to move things on.

- Ask questions like, 'What shall we do now?' 'What is the next step (of the conversation)?'

Check actions your partner has decided to take. Introduce humour if things get too 'heavy'; lightness when things get too dark; warmth when it is needed.

This might seem daunting, but don't be put off by the amount involved in listening. You can use this list for ideas to start with, or to review your efforts afterwards. More important than 'getting it right' is the simple willingness to help the other person; commitment to your speaking partner is the first essential of the relationship. Once you have this then just get started and try some of these ideas, improving as you go.

WORKING WITH YOUR ROLE SET: FINDING ALLIES

To survive and be effective in your organization you need allies as well as friends. You will probably find some of these allies among your close colleagues at work - the members of your role set. This is the term applied to those people who occupy the roles or positions which relate directly to your role as manager, partner, friend or whatever. They include your boss, any colleagues with whom you have 'sideways' relationships and the people who report to you and for whom you are responsible, as well as your spouse, partner, children, family friends.

In a role set everyone has obligations to, and expectations of, the others. You expect your boss to provide you with access to resources, a higher level of decision, to represent you elsewhere and so on. In return you have obligations to your boss - to manage a particular section, to report regularly and keep information flowing upwards and so on. This reciprocal pattern of obligations and expectations will apply to all the other people in your role set, and also to people outside work.

People in this web of relationships are in the best position to judge the performance, skills, abilities and effectiveness of any person in the middle - which is why 360 degree feedback methods have come into use. It takes some courage to enlist the people around you at work in your self-managing efforts, but it may be that, if you take the initiative, some of them may become interested too. Others will become curious and want to know what you think of them and their performance on particular tasks, in certain meetings, on various aspects of your work together.

Role set analysis

The first task is to identify the people in your role set. The example below is of a work-based set, but you can focus on any set - outside work or inside and outside. Draw a circle in the middle of a piece of paper to represent your work role and write your name and job title underneath. Around this centre circle, draw other circles to represent the 'significant others' in your job role set - those with whom you have regular contact, who make demands on you and have expectations of you. Here is an example of the role set of an office manager.

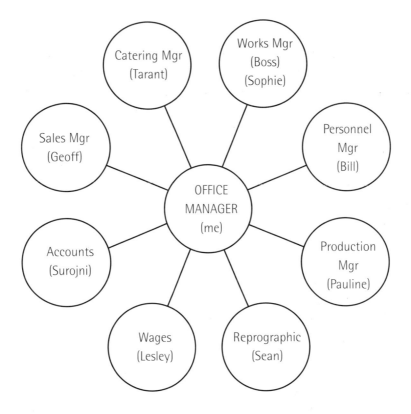

Figure 7.2. : The Role Set of an Office Manager

This is a simple example, you can put in as many people as you like, indicating closeness or regularity of contact by putting the circles near to yours or further away. The next step is deciding how to enlist these people to help you manage yourself. You need to give some thought to the best way of doing this because whatever you do will change established relationships. You may have to face barriers to discussion and plain speaking as a result of differences in rank or grade; managing upwards, sideways and downwards.

Here are three ideas for working with your role set: dealing with expectations; curbside conferences; and role set surveys.

My expectations / your expectations

Arrange to meet one to one with the members of your role set who you think might be willing to give you useful information. For each meeting, prepare by jotting down the expectations that you think that person has of you in your job and, in another column, the expectations you have of them. Ask the other person to do the same, so that they are similarly prepared. For example, if you were the office manager preparing to meet with Surojni, the accounts supervisor, your notes might look like this:

My Expectations/Your Expectations

	Expectations of me	My expectations of her
Accounts supervisor (Sarojni)	1. Fair loading of work. 2. Support for her actions with her people. 3. Personal support - to be available to listen. 4. To get resources for our departments. … and so on…	1. Achieve work targets. 2. Deal with her own people problems. 3. Keep me informed about likely delays, trouble spots etc. 4. Take initiatives -but let me know … and so on…

When you meet with the person concerned, you could simply exchange notes or agree to work down your two lists taking it in turns to introduce an expectation and discussing what it means. It depends on your relationship with that person and what it takes to get a good discussion going in which new information is exchanged, trust is developed, and personal change is made possible. The points made earlier about talking, listening and responding all apply to this exchange, and if you can manage it well then you will perhaps have found a new speaking partner.

Curbside conferences

This is a more specific contract that you set up for a particular issue or occasion. Supposing you were worried about a large meeting at which you had to speak or unsure about your negotiating skills with people from another organization. Ask one of your role set members in the same meeting or in a position to observe you negotiating to help you learn from the action. Ask this person or persons to look for particular things, to check any doubts you might have about your own performance. For example, what happens when you get lost or confused in a talk or what happens when the other person becomes aggressive, and so on.

Next arrange a quick session afterwards to get that person's feedback on those points. The term 'curbside conference' comes from sales training where, after each call, you get immediate feedback to make you think about how you will handle the next encounter. This incorporates the best rules of skill development - try something with an observer watching, get immediate feedback, think how you will do it next and try this out.

Role set survey

A third idea is to survey all the members of your role set on how they see you operating or how they view the services offered by your department. This is your own 360 degree feedback device. Send out a letter with an attached questionnaire requesting feedback on various aspects of your performance. It may be best to prepare people for receiving this by speaking to them all in advance and telling them what you intend and why. Because of the relatively formal nature of the letter and questionnaire, you may get a better response if you ask about the performance of your section or department, and in this case you need to discuss this with any other members of the departmental staff first. A suitable letter and questionnaire might look like this:

Dear ...,

As you know, I'm trying to develop the services which the office supplies to the organization as a whole, and I'd like your views on what we do at the moment and any thoughts you might have on what we could do to improve the level of service.

I enclose a brief questionnaire and I'd be very pleased if you could return it to me by the end of this month.

Yours truly,

The questionnaire could include such questions as:

1. What services do you expect from the office?
2. For each of the services you have listed in (1) above, please comment on each in terms of quality, grading it 'excellent', 'good', 'fair' or 'poor'.
3. What services which we currently do not provide would you like to see us put on in future?
4. What words would you use to describe the office? For example, busy, relaxed, friendly, helpful, unhelpful, slow, bureaucratic, flexible, customer-oriented, time-wasters, skilful, useless etc. Please pick from these and add your own to give as full a picture as possible.
5. What words would you use to describe the management style of the office? For example, autocratic, democratic, consultative, distant, friendly, relaxed, task-oriented, people-centred etc. Please add words of your own.

Such questions will obviously give you details about the performance of your section rather than personal data about you. However it can create an opportunity to go and talk in more detail with respondents. Even if the data is not that good, the exercise might be worthwhile just in terms of making these openings. It is much easier to ask, 'Could we talk about your comments to my survey questions?' than it is to go in cold and say, 'What do you think of the way I manage?'

NETWORKING: MAKING CONTACTS

Networks are informal organizations that exist between people with similar interests; they act as grapevines, conveying gossip and information often much more quickly than formal systems of communication. Everyone knows about 'old boy networks' that help their usually male members get on and get things done. Knowing from whom and from where to get information and help - for example, from front line staff that come into contact with so many people, is one of *the* political skills.

Networks are like string bags; any one point is only connected to four other points, but through these four, each point can reach eight others, and through those twelve more, and so it goes on. Faced by a problem to which we don't have the answer, we call the person most likely to know. He or she may know or not, but, if not, they probably know someone else who does.

It helps to have lots of contacts in any endeavour, and a personal support and development network, with a purpose of mutual help in self-management, can operate for you in a similar way to any other network.

Why not check out your support network at this point by working through Activity 14 on p.198 which gives a useful way of thinking about this?

ACTIVITY 14 Page 198

Networking is one of the key skills for self-managers. Though it is normal to have some gaps in your list, having a wide range of people to call upon adds immeasurably to your resourcefulness. You will need all sorts of help, and the bigger and more varied the network you can call on, the better supported you are. Building up and maintaining your support network takes time and in turn you become a source of support, help and information for other people, because you know so many people.

SELF-DEVELOPMENT GROUPS: GETTING COMRADES

Friends, allies and contacts can become comrades if they join with you in a group to tackle the self-managing quest. Though there is no fixed pattern, such groups typically consist of six to ten members, meeting regularly over six months or more. Sometimes they grow out of courses or project teams where people want to carry on working together, at other times self-development groups are 'facilitated' by a trainer or have access to training ideas and resources.

The main requirements are the shared commitment to self-management and a mutual agreement to learn with and from each other. The group might be an oasis to retreat to, or a pressure cooker for development; or it might be both at different times.

Here are some guidelines for setting up and managing a self-development group. The main phases of a group's life are:

1. setting up and recruiting

2. getting started - the first meeting

3. choosing a focus

4. decision-making

5. maintaining energy and commitment

6. helpful actions

7. reviewing progress

8. closing down.

Because we are used to other people organizing our learning and development for us, setting up your own self-development group might seem a daunting prospect. Depending on how you feel, you may be able to enlist the help of your management development or training people to help you in this, but think carefully about this - above all, the purpose of a self-development group is to be self-directing.

Setting up and recruiting

Groups members can come from the same organization, from professional networks or from any common interest group. Here are three ways of making contact with other, interested people.

A general announcement

Put a notice on a board or in a newsletter inviting others to contact you or join you for a discussion meeting. Make this an open meeting with no obligation to join. This gives everyone a chance to ask questions and make up their own minds.

A personal invitation to a specific person

If you know three or four people who might like this sort of experience you can contact them personally and ask them to bring one other person along to the first meeting. People must feel free to join the group or not; voluntary commitment is what makes self-management groups work and 'invitations' can sometimes pressurize people, so be careful.

An invitation by letter

The following is an example.

> Dear ...,
> This is to invite you to a discussion meeting in my office on 22 January at 10 am to consider setting up a self-development group. As you know, I have been working on improving my managing skills and I'd like to start meeting with a group of interested people. I think a small

group of six or eight meeting perhaps every three weeks for a few hours to share ideas, learn new skills and generally tackle problems facing us, could be of mutual benefit. Please do come.

Yours truly,

PS: This is a 'no obligation' meeting; I want everyone to feel free to decide to join or not - after talking about it, it will be OK to say 'No, thanks, not for me at this time'.

Getting started: the first meeting

Once you've held your 'no obligation' meeting and got at least five or six people committed, the next step is to break the ice and begin to establish openness and trust and the ground rules on which the group will operate. The obvious way to start is to get people to share things about themselves - their lives, their interests and their concerns or problems. Here are three ways to get started on sharing information.

Introduction pairs

People pair off and interview each other, asking each other about work, home, hobbies, beliefs, why they have come to the group and so on. After 10 or 15 minutes each way, the group re-forms and each member introduces their partner rather than themselves to the group, for example, 'I've been talking to Jack who is ...' This is a good way to introduce all members to the whole group.

Glimpses

First, each person writes down ten important things about themselves. Then in turn each comes to the blackboard or flipchart and writes up the items on their list saying a bit about them and explaining them as they go along. Other people ask questions for clarification.

What sort of people emerge from these glimpses? Discuss how different people present themselves - who is complimentary and who is a self-denigrator and so on.

A letter to the group

Everyone writes a letter addressed to the group introducing themselves. The letter can be in the first person, introducing him or herself: 'My name is ..., I am ...' and so on, or in the third person as though the writer were describing somebody else like in giving reference for them: 'I am writing to introduce... He/ She is ...' . When the letters have been written, each person takes it in turn to read theirs out to the group. Alternatively, the letters can be folded into a hat and distributed so that everyone reads out one, which is not their own, omitting the name as they do so. This can be good fun, and can lead into a discussion about how we see and present ourselves to other people.

Ground Rules

Ground rules are the guidelines or principles which govern the way a group works. All groups operate to ground rules whether these are acknowledged or not. In management meetings these are set by tradition, culture or the senior person's preference. A self-development group should establish its own and operate to any ground rules which members agree upon.

Each person writes down the way they want the group to operate. What rules should apply to behaviour inside and outside group meetings? One person then writes all of these on a flipchart. Discuss all the proposals as they go up and then choose some of them - not more than seven or eight - to guide the group from now on.

You can choose any rules that you can agree on. Whatever works for a particular group are the right rules. As an example, the areas commonly covered by ground rules are:

- Confidentiality (This often comes out first, but what does it mean? Can I talk about my thoughts and feelings to others? Disclose this to my mentor? 'Confidentiality' usually needs clarification.)

- A safe place to admit needs, weaknesses and mistakes

- Commitment to attending

- Equal sharing of time

- Listening - to everyone

- Support members in what they want to do

- Challenge people but without making judgements

- Punctuality - starting and finishing on time.

Groups might also have rules about how or when or where to meet, about shared actions, celebrating achievements or anything else that is important to them. The rules should be re-visited at the second meeting and checked from time to time for their continuing appropriateness and effectiveness.

Choosing a focus

As well as getting to know one another, you will probably want to talk at the first meeting about what to work on or the focus for the group. Self-management groups can focus on one or more of the following:

- Work issues and problems.

- Structured exercises, case studies, visiting speakers etc - brought along by members to look at issues at work or at home.

- Personal Development Plans - where the group helps people develop and fulfill their plans.

- Biography work - where careers or life planning forms the focus.

- Group processes - studying the 'here and now' issues in this group - (including communication, decision-making).

Below are two ways to help you arrive at a focus. You may not need them if people are willing and able to put their issues straight on the table - although they could still act as 'warm up' exercises.

Needs and offers

Each person takes two postcards, one for 'needs' and one for 'offers', and writes down three needs they have as a manager and/or as a person; and three offers of knowledge, skill, help they could make to other group members. The postcards are then pinned on the wall under 'Help Wanted' and 'Help Offered' notices. Are there any matching needs and offers? Or any common needs? Or any patterns? The group can begin work by focusing on any person(s) with any need(s).

Critical incidents

Members agree to note down, once each day between now and the next meeting, 'the most difficult managerial task/problem I have tackled today'. At the next meeting, people take it in turn to read these out and explain how they dealt with them. Others can say how they tackle similar issues.

Decision making

Deciding where to start and what to do next can be difficult. Some people do not mind what happens next, while others may pull in different directions. Sorting this out and arriving at a consensus can leave some people impatient or even frustrated. Therefore, try to:

- Make sure everyone says what he or she wants.

- Write all possible options on a flipchart to aid personal choices and a collective decision.

- Do not assume that silence means consent. It often doesn't.

- Do review decisions made at the end of the session - how do we feel about them?

A good group aims to meet the needs of all its members; if we do

X now, we can do Y at the next meeting.

Maintaining energy and commitment

As in life, energy will go up and down. Don't expect high energy in the group all the time; being quiet and reflective is necessary and just as valuable at times. However, if you feel energy or commitment are flagging, don't let it drag on, raise the question. Say that you feel 'bored' or 'low' and ask how others feel. If others feel as you do, try a different activity, a change of pace or place. Go for coffee, a walk, or something.

Helpful actions

Is help helpful? A main purpose of self-development groups is to help oneself and each other but this isn't always easy. There is an old joke that goes, 'If things don't improve soon, I shall have to ask you to stop helping me!' Before thinking about active help consider these three essential 'human rights' for people in self-management groups:

- the right to speak

- the right to be listened to

- the right to remain silent.

These three 'rights' are the foundations for each participant. Everyone should feel able to speak freely and take up 'air time'. Everyone should have the right to sympathetic listening and questioning to enable them to express what they want to say. Finally, each person should have the right to remain silent about those things they don't want to speak about or answer. Other kinds of useful behaviour in most groups includes the following.

Listening
This is perhaps the most useful thing we can do for another person. Give people as much time to speak as they want. In a

normal meeting we follow the topic with everybody chipping in, but in a self-development group we follow the person. Have they finished speaking? Have they had enough time? Do they want to go further? When is it time to move on to the next person? It can be hard to be the focus of the group's attention at first and people may say things like, 'I think it is someone else's turn now' when they mean, 'I'm finding this difficult, can someone help'.

Boundaries
Respect your own and other people's boundaries: they need their defences just as much as you. Yet sometimes people need a little push when they want to go a bit further, say a bit more.

Support and challenge
In combination they make for the best climate for development. Warm baths of support are lovely for a while, but a group can become too safe; challenges to established ways of thinking and acting are essential but individuals can only take so much of them. How is the balance between support and challenge in the group?

Silences
Don't rush into filling them. A silence may allow someone to sort something out in a way which talking can't. Learn to value them.

Commitment to action before the next meeting
Close the meeting by each person saying what they intend to do as a result of the group discussion. Few things are more encouraging to people and to groups than that their efforts are having an influence. At the next meeting check back and find out what happened to these intentions. What can be learned from these outcomes?

Reviewing progress

It is a good idea - perhaps every three or four meetings - to check direction and progress. If there are concerns about energy, commitment or whether the group is meeting people's needs then this might be a good time to take stock.

There are several ways of doing this. The simplest is to spend the last half hour of a meeting with each person giving their evaluation and thoughts so far. Another way is to 'brainstorm' a joint list of what is helping the group and what is hindering. To give more time for reflection you could use a simple questionnaire, for example as follows.

1. What are you getting from these group sessions?

2. What are you giving to other members?

3. Is the level of trust in the group high or low?

4. Does everyone participate and get a fair share of 'air time'?

5. Does the group have a clear sense of purpose?

6. Taking each member of the group in turn, what would you like to see them continue to do, stop doing or start doing?

7. What would you like to see changed or done differently?

When each person has completed this, the answers can be collated and read out. Alternatively you can just discuss the questions without revealing detailed answers, now that everyone has thought about the key issues and questions. Finally, a warning note: there is sometimes a tendency to rush to evaluation too early. If evaluation is to be developmental rather than destructive, it must help both in reflecting on what has happened and moving on to the next stage.

Closing down and making a good end

Often a very difficult thing to do. Some members may want to continue while others don't. The worst thing to happen is a 'creeping death' as members drop off one by one. Far better to choose and finish on a given date with a celebration - a meal or a party - to mark the occasion.

At this last meeting do a full review of what members have

gained, and allow time for some last messages between people. Is there any unfinished business? Dealing with these matters and the whole question of closing may make some people feel awkward and want to avoid it, but it is very important to close properly. A good end should be made so that people are free to move on in their lives without the burden of unfinished business.

CONCLUSION

Working with people as speaking partners, in role sets, and networks helps reduce the isolation of going it alone. Others help us release our own energy and overcome our tendencies to get blocked, demoralized or stuck in the grooves and ruts of work organizations. The effect of some people developing or taking initiatives to manage themselves is very contagious. When two or three or more band together for these purposes they create warm spots in the organization which begin to heat up the rest. The opposite is also true - that the influence of lots of stuck, isolated or non-developing people freezes it for others.

Creating a supportive self-development climate in the whole organization is the natural extension of managing yourself with the help of other people. The next chapter takes the theme of how to build the learning organization.

8 Managing Yourself Within the Organization

By working with your friends, allies, contacts and comrades you are already well on the way to managing yourself within the organization. Beyond personal connections, there are some wider aspects to take into account. The first aspect is the organization's stage of development. Organizations can be seen as developing through a series of stages or phases, each characterized by particular needs or tasks to be accomplished, which in turn make different demands upon the people concerned. Secondly, is your organization a learning organization? Does it put learning at the centre of its strategy and operations? Thirdly, one way of assessing your organization as a learning company is by looking at the characteristics and quality of the organizational climate. How well does this climate support you and others from a self-management perspective? Are people's efforts to make choices and take initiatives discouraged or rewarded? A supportive climate makes a huge difference. Fourthly and finally, what can you do to manage yourself in a non-learning organization, one with a non-supportive organizational climate? Managing yourself is more difficult under these circumstances, so how can you manage to take initiatives and find ways of keeping up your courage and enthusiasm?

Managing yourself within the organization is another step along the road begun in Chapter 1; from managing me first and working outwards to other people. In company with others, self-developing people can help bring about the learning organization.

ORGANIZATIONS AS LIVING ORGANISMS

As living collective organisms, organizations can be said to have a biography with a birth, stages of development or maturity and, finally, a death. Organizations are formed from three forces:

- *Ideas* - the visions and images that founders seek to realize and which are passed on to succeeding generations to re-create

- *Phase* - the life stage of the company, e.g. infant, pioneer, rational, overripe bureaucracy, dying

- *Era* - the economic, social, political and cultural context.

The current *era* for most organizations is characterized by competitiveness and unprecedented change; and this has led to the idea of the learning company or learning organization (of which more below). *Ideas* are the major source of organizational difference and personality. Even in the same business, organizations have very different core ideas and purposes. For example, although the two may share many purposes in common, an Oxford college will conceive of itself very differently from a new university.

Another factor that makes a difference is the organization's current *phase* of development. Organizations are commonly personalized as being strong or weak, young or old, informal or cold and, like people, some organizations, vibrant and dynamic in their youth, get stuck and lose their way whilst others manage to renew their energy and purpose.

Now think for a moment about your organization as if it were a person with its own individual needs for development. How do you see your organization as a person? To consider the age and stage of development of your organization, turn now to Activity 15 on p.200.

ACTIVITY 15 Page 200

WHAT IS YOUR ORGANIZATION'S STAGE OF DEVELOPMENT?

Although they are unique there are some typical problems and questions that most organizations seem to face at certain times. These relate to particular stages or phases of development. For example, a company that establishes standard rules and systems to create a consistency of quality and treatment later begins to experience problems of rigidity, lack of motivation and complaints from unit managers about their lack of autonomy. When these problems reach a significant level they have to be dealt with, and these actions, while resolving the old problems, also create the conditions in which new ones will arise.

Below the six typical stages in the life cycle of the organization are set out, together with the problems and issues that tend to arise at each. Where is your organization and what are its current problems and tasks?

First stage of development: the new business

Starting a new organization, either as an independent entrepreneur, or as in a new department or section within an existing enterprise.

Typical tasks and problems

- What is the vision of the new organization?

- What will it look like, what will it do, what will it feel like?

- How can this version be turned into action?

- What resources are needed? Where will the premises,

equipment, money and people come from?

- How can we market ourselves and begin to trade with the wider world?

Second stage: the pioneer organization

Small with a dynamic, pioneering leader or initiating group.

Typical tasks and problems

- Do we continue to be small or grow larger?

- If we expand, what new systems are needed to cope with increased business?

- How will new people be integrated? How will the initiators and the 'in-comers' work together?

- Succession: who can replace the leader or initiators? Is a new style of leadership needed?

Third stage: expanding organization

The independent enterprise or section gets complex and bigger.

Typical tasks and problems

- Doubts arise about the pioneers. There are questions about competence and grumbles about authoritarianism. Times are changing and the way we used to do things is no longer appropriate.

- What new systems are needed to bring order to the hitherto creative chaos?

- How can 'scientific management' methods be implemented to ensure standardization, consistency and control?

- What specialist functions need to be established, e.g. sales, administration, research, personnel?

Fourth stage: the established organization

Typically exists where there has been formalization for some time, with written procedures and logical, scientific methods applied to most aspects of its functioning.

Typical tasks and problems

- How can we deal with the problems of rigidity and inflexibility, red tape and bureaucracy that have set in?

- Why is there so much apathy and low motivation about?

- What can be done about the rivalry and competition between departments and functions that should be spent on production, sales and competing in the market?

- Can we decentralize and differentiate - to give more autonomy?

Fifth stage: the wilderness organization

One which has lost its way and become remote from the outside world. Increasingly likely with advancing age and size, especially in the case of bureaucracies.

Typical tasks and problems

- How can change our relationship with our customers and clients? Should we have new clients?
- Can we decentralize and differentiate to meet customer needs?
- How can we change our unhealthy view that sees the outside world, including our customers, business partners, community

and environment as 'enemies' or obstructions to be bullied, cajoled and overcome, by trickery and sharp practice, if necessary?

- What should be our new moral purpose? What would build a healthy relationship, i.e. one of the mutually advantageous collaboration with other stakeholders, including the government, customers, and community.

Sixth stage: the dying organization

One that has failed or gone bankrupt, or whose initial mission is finished and which can or should no longer continue.

Typical tasks and problems

- Can anything be done to reverse the failure?

- Can the organization be rescued through merger, surgery, buyout or other means, to create new life, a new mission and a fresh start?

- Should anything be done to reverse the death process, or is this natural and indeed desirable?

- What can be done to come to a good end? How can closing down be made as positive and as pain-free as possible.

- What are the moral obligations to the stakeholders - employees, customers, shareholders and community?

- What new seeds can spring from the husk of the old organization?

What are the implications of your organization's current stage of development for you? How can you survive and protect yourself in this dynamic environment and prepare and develop in order to make a contribution to some of the critical tasks at this time? To start to answer these questions begin by locating your organization in terms of the above stages of development.

- In broad terms, which description of typical tasks and problems best fits your organization or department?

- What are the specific issues which face your organization - problems to overcome or tasks to be accomplished?

- Some have been suggested, but list your own specific items.

- Now put against each in your list, the qualities or skills of people and perhaps the ways of working that will help with these tasks. Show these lists to some other people to get an idea of how they see the situation.

Thinking about these should give you a better idea of where your organization is and where you fit in. It should also tell you whether your abilities and ways of working belong more to the past, present or future. A few examples will illustrate this.

In the early stages of starting up a new business, people are needed with imagination and commitment who don't mind doing all sorts of tasks, who will work all hours and are prepared to see rewards in the future. These are often inventive people who can turn their hands to whatever comes up and respond flexibly and quickly. After a time, if operations get bigger, more order and systems are needed. This means that people with quite different qualities are required - specialists who can divide work and establish tight controls and standards over work areas. Professional competence replaces the all-rounders.

Later, the *established organization* needs people who can shake up structures that have become rigid due to demarcation, division of labour, specialization and bureaucracy. Such individuals have 'people skills', can work across boundaries and are good trainers and negotiators. In the *wilderness organization* inward-lookingness has become a problem and people who can look outside, work into the community and change the relationship between the organization and its wider world are urgently needed. If the organization reaches a terminal stage, counsellors and caretakers become key figures and there is an urgent need for people who can be the midwives of new initiatives.

These few examples show what is appropriate at one time in an organization's development may well not be at another. This helps explain why people can get beached or stuck even in quite senior positions. The 'Peter Principle' holds that such people were promoted until they eventually reached a level of incompetence, but it could be that their skills and abilities were in great demand at a particular time but are now simply less valued and useful as things have moved on. At any given time there will be people whose qualities match the needs of that time, and indeed, those whose time has not yet come. And time will eventually be called on your current skills, unless you are capable of learning new ways of working in the future.

The 'stuckness' problem becomes particularly acute for organizations seeking change or flexibility. Many organizations today face the overriding challenge of how to learn quickly and continuously enough in the face of increasing competition, rapid change and unpredictable circumstances. Managing change and learning has become the priority task in schools, hospitals and cities as much as in business and commerce.

Such organizations have great need for self-developers and seek to balance appropriate bureaucracy with empowering people to develop themselves and take initiatives. A rigid bureaucracy is not a fit place for self-managing people; the climate is such that they never develop in this way, and if they are by chance recruited, they do not survive. Only those organizations aspiring to be learning organisations or something similar are fit to house self-developers.

IS YOUR ORGANIZATION A LEARNING ORGANIZATION?

The pressures for change have exposed the limitations of bureaucratic or autocratic management styles which, even in their supposedly lean and mean versions, are not sensitive or flexible enough to make radical changes or - more importantly - to build up the internal capacity for learning and development to thrive.

Reg Revans has proposed the ecological formula, $L \geq C$, where learning in the organization must be equal to or greater than the rate of environmental change (Revans RW (1998) *ABC of Action*

Learning). If the learning rate inside is less than the rate of external change, then the organization is declining or dying. As change accelerates 'organizational death' comes in many guises through failure, acquisition or merger. It has been suggested that the life expectancy of the average US corporation now is less than 40 years and falling.

According to Peter Senge in *The Fifth Discipline* a learning organization is a place:

> '... where people continually expand their capacity to create the results they truly desire ... where people are continually learning how to learn together ..... where people are continually discovering how they create reality. And how they can change it.'

With our colleague John Burgoyne, (Pedler, Burgoyne and Boydell (1997) *The Learning Company*) we have suggested that the learning company helps all its people develop, but is also able to change itself - and its immediate environment - as a whole. It is:

> '... an organization that facilitates the learning of all its members and consciously transforms itself and its context.'

Pursuing the vision of the learning organization means that the enterprise is taking learning seriously and putting it at the centre of its values and operating processes, making *intentional* use of the learning:

- of individual people

- of teams, groups and units

- functional boundaries, between departments and through status levels

- within the whole organization and,

- with the organization's trading partners and stakeholders.

Do these ideas fit with the aspirations of the people in your organization? Perhaps you have a different way of looking at things? Because the vision and the reality of the learning organization are developed from within there is no blueprint, no single right answer. Such organizations aspire to put learning at the centre of their ways of doing things; action is taken for learning purposes as much as for immediate operational purposes. It's how you do it that counts. (See also Pedler M and Aspinwall K (1998) *A Concise to the Learning Organization.*)

THE CLIMATE IN YOUR ORGANIZATION

One test for the learning organization is by noticing the way it impacts on you. Whether people are encouraged to develop and manage themselves or not depends a lot upon the prevailing climate in your organization. The original sense of this term refers to weather conditions - which support or inhibit particular forms of life. The climate of an organization comes through as a pervasive tone or 'feel' in terms of social and procedural norms. It is composed from many factors including history and traditions, physical environment, products, structures and technologies.

What are the conditions like in your organization in terms of various aspects or dimensions of the learning climate? To gain a measure of how your organizational learning climate supports or inhibits development turn now to Activity 16 on p.201.

MANAGING YOURSELF IN A POOR ORGANIZATIONAL CLIMATE

With a supportive climate most people can take some steps towards managing themselves, but can you do so if you're stuck in a poor climate where people are punished for not conforming to rules, where learning is a low priority and where communications and standards are low? First, there are the basic choices spelt out in Chapter 2. Try thinking about these, working through a mapping exercise in Chapter 2. Can you ...

- change the situation

- change yourself

- leave the situation

- tolerate the situation?

If none of these help, try creating your own micro-climate by finding friends, allies, contacts and comrades as suggested in the last chapter. Just one friend or ally - even if you have to go outside the organization to find them - could transform your circumstances.

A practical reason for taking action on managing yourself - even in the most hostile or infertile climate - stems from the consequences of not doing so. Consider the following story.

CASE STUDY

For twenty-nine years Derek was an accountant with a bank and then he was made redundant. A retiring but clever child, his teachers had tried hard to persuade Derek's parents to let him stay on at school, but Derek's parents had little education of their own and had encouraged the 16-year-old in getting a steady job instead. Derek had enjoyed the job and proved a willing and loyal worker and a first-class professional. The job suited him down to the ground; technically demanding and calling for meticulous work to high standards, he tended to work alone, often staying after hours to finish a job. Derek liked his work, cared little about promotion and concentrated on providing for his family.

When redundancy came it hit him hard. He went into shock and moped around the house. After some time his wife Sheila, needing money and fed up with him, got herself a job and discovered a whole new world. Derek's few pals encouraged him to look for work and to try volunteering. But Derek knew he stood no chance of finding work. He felt useless and hopeless. His work experience had encouraged his natural leanings to be shy and self-absorbed and had not prepared him for finding new work at 45. He was never one for taking initiatives or to choose his own work; he was not a 'people person' and hated telephone conversations of more than two minutes; he had little curiosity or knowledge about the wider world. Socially he had been content to let Sheila do the organizing.

• •

Many conscientious men and women have shared Derek's fate. Their work experience has not helped them develop the skills and capacities needed to help find new work, new methods or new people. In terms of the stage model from Chapter 3 (Table 3.2), they are stuck in Mode 2.

The work that we do forms us - or deforms us - in certain ways. Through work people can develop capacities and abilities to high standards, but the most sobering aspect of Derek's story is that of the bright and able child rendered incurious, lacking in basic social skills, unable to learn new ways by the experience of thirty years of unchanging work. Even qualified professionals are not immune to these dangers, being both highly skilled and, in other ways, potentially disabled, stuck in certain grooves of practice.

Few organizations offer jobs for life these days and those that do are not to be trusted. Instead many talk about enhancing 'employability' in their people. To the work ethic inherited from the Victorians and the twentieth century notion of commitment to the work organization must now be added a self-managing ethic. Accepting that the organization can't be relied upon in this way, frees you to look to your own resources. While working, time and energy also has to be invested in maintaining knowledge and learning new skills. The generalized ability to learn how to learn has to be exercised and kept in trim.

There is a second argument for keeping going whatever the conditions, and this is the moral duty to look after, maintain and develop ourselves - not only for our own sake but for that of others. The urge to development, to awareness, conscious self-management, is not just a practical, sensible thing; it is fuelled by deeper drives. The 'impossible situation' is especially one in which ideas must be kept alive so that there are seeds to be sown when things change - as they always do. Seeds are kept alive in the example and practice of people who have the courage to 'keep keeping on' when the going is difficult. It is in this sense many people feel a duty to make the best of themselves and to make a contribution by seeking to live a good life.

The Buddha taught that the path of human development leads from suffering to enlightenment, and described a path for all human beings to tread. The conditions of the world which weigh heavily, the stuckness, triviality and absurdity felt by people in organizations, in their jobs and their lives, are this suffering which can only be avoided at the cost of unawareness. From this perspective managing yourself serves the higher purpose of making the best of ourselves, for ourselves, for others and for the force of good in the world.

MAKING THE MOST OF IT

In some ways managing yourself is like running your own small business. Keeping going requires an ability to spot openings and opportunities and keeping up the motivation to grasp them and make something of them. It is easy to lose sight of the various openings for self-managing which abound in all organizations. There is a trick of seeing what's on offer that can help you survive, maintain or develop yourself.

What is the organization anyway? Is it the single and reassuring structure of the organization chart, or like a kaleidoscope, does it reflect different faces from different angles? Calling it 'the organization' confers a sense solidity which perhaps only exists for certain purposes or from certain perspectives; the organizational chart is just a map not the actual terrain. In any case you cannot work with an 'organization' but only with people, and each person tends to have a different picture of what the organization is, what its goals and purposes are, where the power lies, what values are important, and so on.

Realizing that your view of the organization is only one of many alternative pictures that exist is the starting point for finding opportunities. A single view creates a prison - a sense of being stuck in the system - whilst opening up to other perceptions creates gaps, loose ends, openings and starting points.

Activity 17 on p.205 provides a way of auditing the organizational structures, activities and processes that may offer openings for you. Try this and then think again about your own strategy.

The poorer your organizational climate, and perhaps the smaller your organization, the fewer openings you will find, but you should discover some possibilities by making a thorough audit. Asking other people, 'What do you do to find out about things here?' or 'What goes on here that I could learn or get support from?' would be good ways to start. (To make the most of learning opportunities at work, see also John Burgoyne, *Developing Yourself, Your Career and Your Organization* (1999)).

When you have found some openings, pick one or two and get started. Do this on the basis of what you feel attracted to and don't worry too much about the logic. Any effort at managing yourself needs energy or motivation first; warmth comes before light. When you get the inkling of a new idea, nurture it, warm it up by thinking about it, talk about it to anyone who will listen. Sometimes this may take quite a time but you've already made an important start, in nurturing a small seed. Then, when you're ready, take the next steps to bring the idea to light in some activity. This is the process of self-managing.

Activities

Activity 1: Inside/Outside

The purpose of this Activity is to help you think about the way you are currently managing yourself. Jot down your answers in the space below or in your own 'managing myself' journal.

First recall four or five occasions when you think you managed something or somebody really well.

From Mike Pedler and Tom Boydell (1999) *Managing Yourself*, Lemos & Crane, London

Next, do the same for four or five occasions when you did pretty badly.

Now, for each of those occasions, good and bad, can you recall how you felt? Were you fully in control, doing what you wanted, saying just what you intended to say, handling your feelings rather than allowing them to overwhelm you? Or were you out of control, losing your temper, not able to express yourself properly, failing to find the right words that you knew were there somewhere but couldn't get hold of?

There will probably be a link between these events. When you were in control, in charge, consciously managing yourself, that's when things went well. And when you lost control of yourself that's when you lost control of the situation.

From Mike Pedler and Tom Boydell (1999) *Managing Yourself*, Lemos & Crane, London

Activity 2: How well am I doing?

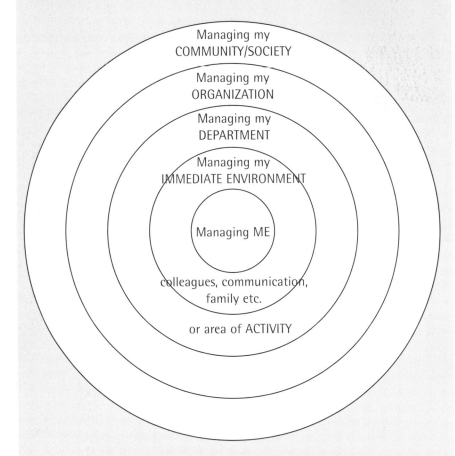

Managing my
COMMUNITY/SOCIETY

Managing my
ORGANIZATION

Managing my
DEPARTMENT

Managing my
IMMEDIATE ENVIRONMENT

Managing ME

colleagues, communication,
family etc.

or area of ACTIVITY

Managing from the inside out

*Looking at the diagram above consider yourself and your world.
First of all write down what is going well in each of the rings.*

From Mike Pedler and Tom Boydell (1999) *Managing Yourself,* Lemos & Crane, London

- What's good about the way you're managing yourself? What are doing with your abilities, skills, talents, physical and mental condition that pleases you?

- Next, what's good about the way you're managing the people and things immediately around you - at work and at home?

- On to the next ring: what's going well in your department or area of activity because of you?

- And finally, what of the outer ring? Can you say that you are making any contribution to your community - what are you putting into it, how are you helping to manage it?

Now look at the other side of the coin. What's not so good in each of those circles? In what ways are you not doing such a good job of managing them? What pressures, worries, unresolved issues are you aware of?

From Mike Pedler and Tom Boydell (1999) *Managing Yourself*, Lemos & Crane, London

The aim of this exercise is to help you to think about your own survival experiences.

Recall three or four occasions in your life when you were fighting hard to survive. On each occasion:

(a) How did you feel at the time, what was it that kept you going?
(b) What was the longer term effect on you?
(c) Were you in any way different after this time?
(d) How did it affect other people around you, at work and/or at home?

1.

2.

3.

4.

From Mike Pedler and Tom Boydell (1999) *Managing Yourself,* Lemos & Crane, London

Activity 4: The ways you take action questionnaire

1. How do you decide on priorities, choose between competing aims and goals?
- What factors do you take into account? Are there other factors that you ignore, but that might usefully be taken into account? Can you illustrate with examples?

2. When making a decision, how do you generate alternative courses of action?
- How do you decided or choose between these alternatives? What factors do you take into account? And what other possible factors?

3. What have been the two or three most difficult decisions you have made in the past twelve months?
- Why were these difficult? What and who were involved? How did you go about it? What do you now think about the way you handled it? What are your feelings about what happened?

4. Can you see any patterns in the way you respond to particular types of decision-making situations?

5. How do you feel when you encounter setbacks, when what you are doing doesn't seem to be going to well, when the going gets tough?
- What effects do these feelings have?

6. Looking at your answers to these questions, do you think others would agree that this is how you are?
- Do they see you in the same way as you see yourself? Are you sure? Can you find out?

7. What are your thoughts as a result of looking at - or better still, attempting to answer these questions?
- How are your feelings? Do you want to do anything as a result? If not, why not? What are you actually going to do?

Activity 5: Modes of managing questionnaire

Below are fifty statements about yourself and the way you manage. For each statement, allocate points as follows:

1 point: if it is completely untrue of you; you never think or act in that way.

2 points: if it is somewhat true of you; you sometimes think or act in that way.

3 points: if it is quite like you; you fairly often think or act in that way.

4 points: if it is very much like you; you think or act in that way most of the time.

At the end of the questionnaire on p.184 you will find a table made up of 50 boxes - a numbered box for each of the statements 1-50; enter the points (1 to 4) that you have scored yourself for each item in the appropriate box.

1. I base decisions on established rules and regulations.

2. I try to keep reasonably well in with the powers that be.

3. I think that I have a contribution to make to the way that things are done around here.

4. I keep open-minded and take into account any views that other people may have, especially those that seem to differ from or contradict my own.

5. I feel that I know the answer to the question, 'Why on earth am I here?'

From Mike Pedler and Tom Boydell (1999) *Managing Yourself*, Lemos & Crane, London

6. I don't think you should allow feelings to affect the way you do things.

7. I try to find out about the way we do things - who decided it, when and why.

8. A manager's job is to manage.

9. I try to ensure that I have an accurate picture of how others see me.

10. I am committed to a particular idea or philosophy of life.

11. When I am doing something unpleasant, I try to switch off my feelings and wishes and just concentrate on the established rules or procedures.

12. I like to have an explanation of the way we do things.

13. I base decisions on logical, rational thought.

14. I have a strange feeling that everything and everybody are somehow connected.

15. There are some issues and principles to which I am prepared to give priority over my own personal success and ambition.

16. I like to do things by the book.

17. I like to become really proficient in certain specific areas.

18. I go to others for their opinions, and then take these into account when coming to my own decision.

From Mike Pedler and Tom Boydell (1999) *Managing Yourself*, Lemos & Crane, London

19. You should take feelings as well as facts into account when making decisions.

20. I wonder if I'm making a really useful contribution to the world.

21. When something goes wrong, or I make a mistake, I'll either refer back to the procedures or ask for instructions.

22. If I didn't agree with what was expected of me, I would still do it rather than risk rocking the boat.

23. I like to think things out for myself rather than rely on other people's decisions or explanations.

24. When making decisions, I try to put myself in the place of the other people who are involved and affected and imagine how they will feel.

25. I know what it is that I have to give to the world.

26. I'm at a loss when something new or unexpected turns up.

27. I think that you've got to be clear-cut and decide things one way or the other.

28. I am developing my own way or style of doing things.

29. I base decisions on intuitive feelings for what's involved.

30. I have a degree of dedication to some more important cause than my own development.

From Mike Pedler and Tom Boydell (1999) *Managing Yourself*, Lemos & Crane, London

31. A manager's job is to issue instructions and see that they are carried out.

32. I sometimes have ideas that I think wouldn't be acceptable around here, so I keep them to myself.

33. I look for new experiences, even though these may be difficult and involve uncertainty and risk.

34. A manager's job is to enable everybody to manage themselves.

35. I'm prepared to make personal sacrifices for something I feel to be very important, other than my own career or development.

36. I look to others for instructions as to what to do.

37. When a change occurs I go to others who are also involved and ask them what they are going to do.

38. When something goes wrong, or I make a mistake, I try to learn form it and decide what to do next time.

39. I place importance on thinking about what I can do for my subordinates' development as well as for my own.

40. A manager's job is to create a better world for others to live in.

41. I like to have clear-cut guidelines.

42. I find myself wanting to challenge the status quo but don't bother because there's no real point and it will only make life difficult.

43. Sometimes I feel as though my face no longer fits around here.

44. When I am doing something, I am aware of the effect that my own feelings, wishes and prejudices are having on me, and try to take this into account before coming to a final decision.

45. I believe that I have a real contribution to make to society.

46. When I have finished this questionnaire, I'd like an interpretation of my score with instructions on what it means and what I should do about it.

47. When I have finished this questionnaire, I'd like to compare my scores with those of other people.

48. When I have finished this questionnaire I'd like the opportunity to think about what my scores might mean.

49. When I have finished this questionnaire, I would like to think about it in conjunction with what I have gathered about myself from other methods described in this book and elsewhere.

50. When I have finished this questionnaire, I would like to think about what it means about the extent to which I can make a useful contribution to society.

From Mike Pedler and Tom Boydell (1999) *Managing Yourself*, Lemos & Crane, London

Scoring table

1 ☐	2 ☐	3 ☐	4 ☐	5 ☐
6 ☐	7 ☐	8 ☐	9 ☐	10 ☐
11 ☐	12 ☐	13 ☐	14 ☐	15 ☐
16 ☐	17 ☐	18 ☐	19 ☐	20 ☐
21 ☐	22 ☐	23 ☐	24 ☐	25 ☐
26 ☐	27 ☐	28 ☐	29 ☐	30 ☐
31 ☐	32 ☐	33 ☐	34 ☐	35 ☐
36 ☐	37 ☐	38 ☐	39 ☐	40 ☐
41 ☐	42 ☐	43 ☐	44 ☐	45 ☐
46 ☐	47 ☐	48 ☐	49 ☐	50 ☐

TOTAL	☐	☐	☐	☐	☐
MODE 1 ☐	2 ☐	3 ☐	4 ☐	5 ☐	

What, then, does this tell us about you as a manager? Your score from the questionnaire gives you a profile about your repertoire of modes of managing - the higher the score, the more you are operating in that mode. Pages 51-57 explain these Five Modes of Managing. There is a lot of information here and we suggest that you take time to read and re-read it; think about it; discuss it with a partner or in a group.

From Mike Pedler and Tom Boydell (1999) *Managing Yourself*, Lemos & Crane, London

Activity 6: Feedback Questionnaire

Think of the last three or four occasions when you were given the opportunity of learning something about yourself. What did you do? Did you run away from the situation? If so, how did you do so, in what manner? And why?

Or did you stay with it? How did you respond to the information, and to its source? Constructively or negatively?

In each case, what was the end result? What was the effect on you and your development and self-management? And on the other people involved?

From Mike Pedler and Tom Boydell (1999) *Managing Yourself*, Lemos & Crane, London

Activity 7: Knowing yourself open-ended questionnaire

The following questions are not easy and may require considerable thought, so you might want to reflect on some of them for a day or two before attempting a reply. Or you could pick one or two questions for a particular discussion (with a partner or with yourself) and leave others for later. Manage it in the way that suits you best.

PERSONAL VALUES, BELIEFS AND STANDARDS

1. What are your basic beliefs about people, work, family life, politics, morals, your sex and the opposite sex, your country, nationality and race and people of other nationalities and races?

2. What are your basic beliefs about religion, spiritual matters, life and death?

3. Have you always thought and felt like this, or have your beliefs and values changed over time? If so, were these changes sudden, or evolutionary?

4. If you have said that you don't have any beliefs about any of the above matters, then think again. You almost certainly do, even if they are subconscious - perhaps in the form of hidden assumptions.

5. Where any of the above questions make you feel uncomfortable try to identify the source of the discomfort. Become aware of it, and then, if you wish, make a conscious decision not to explore that area if you don't want to.

6. If you really do think that you have no conscious beliefs in any area, how do you feel about that? What, if anything, would you like to do about it?

7. Can you see any inconsistencies in your beliefs? Do any of them contradict each other?

8. Where do your beliefs come from? What are they based on? Who or what influences you in deciding what is right and what is wrong?

9. How do your beliefs and values influence your thinking, your feeling and what you actually do?

10. Think of some situations when you did something in a way that went against your basic beliefs or values. What happened? How did you feel? Why did you act in this way?

11. Looking over your answers to these last questions, how do you think other people would see you? In the same way as you see yourself or not?

12. Finally, looking back over all your answers, what do you think of them? What picture does this give you of yourself? How do you feel about that? What, if anything, do you intend to do about it?

It should go without saying by now that it is perfectly OK to say you are not going to do anything. Any conscious decision, made with due consideration, is part of managing yourself.

Now turn to the next set of questions on p188.

From Mike Pedler and Tom Boydell (1999) *Managing Yourself*, Lemos & Crane, London

(B) KNOWLEDGE ABOUT YOURSELF

13. Write a two or three page description of yourself, in the third person, as though describing somebody else; for example, 'Sharon is a calm person, she is . . .'. What aspects of yourself do you find easy and are comfortable to describe? What are the difficult, uncomfortable or unaware aspects?

14. Choose a colleague or friend and show this description to them. What do they recognize about you? Where do they have a different view? Attach some blank sheets and ask them to add their own views of you.

15. Looking back over your answers to questions 13 and 14, what do you think of them? What picture does this give you of yourself? How do you feel about that? What, if anything, do you intend to do about it?

From Mike Pedler and Tom Boydell (1999) *Managing Yourself*, Lemos & Crane, London

Activity 8 : Valuing and being myself questionnaire

1. How do you feel about yourself, your characteristics, your strengths, weaknesses, about your body, your health, your skills and abilities?

2. How do your feelings about yourself affect you and what you do? Can you think of examples?

3. Imagine that you have been asked to write a character reference for yourself. What do you say?

4. Do you think other people know how you feel about yourself?

5. Do you have any sense of purpose in life - what it is you are here to do?

6. What are your 'natural gifts', and how are you using them? For whose benefit?

7. Draw up an 'influence map', showing sources of influence on you - who or what influences you in what you do and the way you do it? Are any of these pulling in opposite directions? How do you react to all this?

8. Do you think that other people would share this view of you?

9. Looking back over your answers, what do you think of them? What, if anything, are you going to do about them?

From Mike Pedler and Tom Boydell (1999) *Managing Yourself*, Lemos & Crane, London

Activity 9: Skills with people questionnaire

Mark your level of skill with other people. Try for a spread of skill levels and avoid the safety of ticking down the middle of the 'score card' opposite.

Skill

1. Interviewing
2. Speaking in public
3. Selling things
4. Striking up a conversation
5. Serving on a committee
6. Talking about myself/expressing feelings openly
7. Saying what I want
8. Saying 'No'
9. Encouraging others and building them up
10. Working as a team/group member
11. Speaking on the telephone
12. Complaining in a shop/restaurant
13. Giving others 'bad' news
14. Giving others 'good' news
15. Speaking up when I think something is wrong
16. Relating as an equal to authority, e.g. police, teachers
17. Relating as an equal to service workers, e.g. cleaners, clerical, canteen staff
18. Others...

From Mike Pedler and Tom Boydell (1999) *Managing Yourself,* Lemos & Crane, London

Level of skill

	Can't/ Don't do	Apprentice	Competent worker	Craftsman /woman	Artist
1.					
2.					
3.					
4.					
5.					
6.					
7.					
8.					
9.					
10.					
11.					
12.					
13.					
14.					
15.					
16.					
17.					
18.					

Skills involved in dealing with other people are likely to mark out good managing, and it is worth looking at your pattern to see how it has been formed. Again, start with those skills you haven't learned or don't want to learn. Why is this? Is it to do with 'sibling rivalry' or fear of failure? And what about those patterns of independence and dependence?

From Mike Pedler and Tom Boydell (1999) *Managing Yourself,* Lemos & Crane, London

Choose a skill you have learned at some point in the past. Any skill will do - perhaps one from Activity 9.

- Think back to when you didn't have this skill. What was life like then? How did you feel about yourself? Who did you know who did have this skill? How did you see them in relation to yourself?

- Next, what made you choose to learn this skill? Where did the motivation come from?

- Next, think back to how you recognized what this skill meant in practice. How did you get a picture of what skilled performance was? Did you have a model to help - perhaps a friend or relative who served as an example of a competent worker or craftsperson?

- Next, what target or goal did you set? How did you do this?

- Next, how much practising did you do? How did you feel when you had to practise? Was it enjoyable, tedious, hard work?

- Finally, did you get feedback on your performance? Who from? Did you feel supported and encouraged by other people when you were trying to learn the skill or not? What effect did this have?

From Mike Pedler and Tom Boydell (1999) *Managing Yourself*, Lemos & Crane, London

Activity 11: Behaviour at work quiz

Circle the number on each of the following 8 scales that best characterises your usual response or behaviour, i.e. 1 or 5 if you are very like the behaviour described at either end; 2 or 4 if you lean towards this one or that; and 3 if you're genuinely in balance between the two poles - but don't use this middle position more than once or twice.

Are you.../do you...:

1. Casual about timekeeping	1 2 3 4 5	Punctual, never late
2. Do things at easy pace	1 2 3 4 5	Do things quickly (eat, walk, move etc)
3. Never rushed, even under pressure	1 2 3 4 5	Always rushing about
4. Take time out to think and relax	1 2 3 4 5	Never stop to think; feel guilty about relaxing at work
5. Do one thing at a time	1 2 3 4 5	Keep several 'balls in the air' at once
6. Uncompetitive, avoid conflict	1 2 3 4 5	Very competitive, relish combat
7. Feel as though there's plenty of time	1 2 3 4 5	Always feel a sense of urgency
8. Have many interests; talk about many topics	1 2 3 4 5	Mainly interested in work and talk a lot about it

Now add up all the circled numbers for your total score.

From Mike Pedler and Tom Boydell (1999) *Managing Yourself*, Lemos & Crane, London

Activity 12: My destructive habits quiz

Here are some habits that are actually or potentially damaging to your health. Continuing with these habits is self-destructive because each of us can control them. How much self-destruction do you indulge in? Put a tick in the appropriate column for each item

	I do this regularly	I do this sometimes	I never do this
1. Overeating - eating past the point of feeling well			
2. Eating the 'wrong' things - whatever they are			
3. Smoking			
4. Drinking more than is safe or necessary			
5. Using lifts instead of climbing stairs			
6. Driving distances of less than half a mile			
7. Not wearing my seat belt when driving			

From Mike Pedler and Tom Boydell (1999) *Managing Yourself*, Lemos & Crane, London

	I do this regularly	I do this sometimes	I never do this
8. Bottling up anger, pain, grief and not telling anyone about it			
9. Harbouring suspicions, fears, anxieties and not checking them out			
10. Never giving myself a break from work, duty, responsibilities			
11.			
12.			

How many ticks do you have in each of the three columns? Given that human beings show a typical inventiveness for self-destruction - you should be able to add at least a couple of your own particular habits to the list.

From Mike Pedler and Tom Boydell (1999) *Managing Yourself,* Lemos & Crane, London

Activity 13: Looking after yourself questionnaire

How do you deal with stressful situations? Survival and development depend upon your repertoire of coping mechanisms. Tick any of the following that you do:

1. Build up resistance through regular sleep, exercise and a healthy diet? ☐

2. Talk things through with your partner? ☐

3. Talk things through with our boss or colleagues? ☐

4. Withdraw physically from the stressful situation? ☐

5. Practise relaxing or meditating? ☐

6. Give yourself breaks and treats when you need them? ☐

7. Strictly compartmentalize work and home life? ☐

8. Change to a different work activity? ☐

9. Change to a different non-work activity that engrosses you? ☐

10. Analyse the situation and plan a new strategy? ☐

11. Work harder and take work home? ☐

12. ☐

13. ☐

From Mike Pedler and Tom Boydell (1999) *Managing Yourself,* Lemos & Crane, London

Score 2 points for each of the first 7 you ticked, and 1 point for any of the last 4 ticked.

The differential scoring system is based on the fact that the top seven coping mechanisms are generally reckoned to be better for you, although this varies from person to person. Of course this is not a complete list - are there any others you use? If so, award yourself 1 to 3 points depending upon how good this method is for you.

If you scored 12 points or more, then you have a good repertoire of coping skills; you may still end up stressed but you do know how to get help and to look after yourself.

If you scored between 6 and 12 points, you can cope to some extent, but you need more practise to survive and develop more as a manager.

Less than 6 points? Do you need help from someone who is good at coping to act as coach or counsellor?

From Mike Pedler and Tom Boydell (1999) *Managing Yourself*, Lemos & Crane, London

Begin by identifying the extent and membership of your support network. The table below lists some valuable dimensions of support. Write down against these the names of the people you can call on for help on each dimension. Who does these things for you?

Dimensions of support	Names of people you can go to for this kind of support and help	
	At work	Outside work
Who... ... do I enjoy chatting with?		
... cheers me up?		
... makes me feel competent and valued?		
... can I discuss my self-management with?		
... can I talk to about the activities in this book?		
... can I share good news with?		
... can I share bad news with?		
... do I get useful information from?		

From Mike Pedler and Tom Boydell (1999) *Managing Yourself*, Lemos & Crane, London

Dimensions of support	Names of people you can go to for this kind of support and help	
	At work	Outside work
... gives me feedback?		
... challenges me to action?		
... can I depend on in a crisis?		

Look at your list of names. Are there many gaps? Do you get all your support at home and not at work or vice versa? Do you rely heavily on one or two people or have you got a wide spread of people in your network?

From Mike Pedler and Tom Boydell (1999) *Managing Yourself*, Lemos & Crane, London

Activity 15: Ages and stages

Ignoring for the moment your organization's actual age, which of the following would you say best characterized its current stage of development:

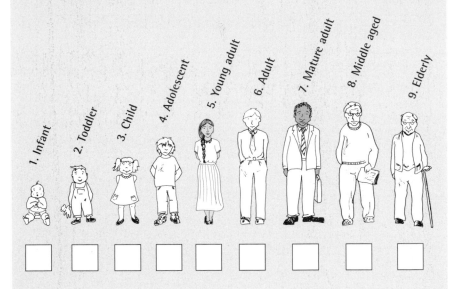

1. Infant 2. Toddler 3. Child 4. Adolescent 5. Young adult 6. Adult 7. Mature adult 8. Middle aged 9. Elderly

1. What stage was the organization at five or ten years ago?

2. What will it be five or ten years from now?

3. Is your organization developing or is it just getting older?

From Mike Pedler and Tom Boydell (1999) *Managing Yourself*, Lemos & Crane, London

Activity 16: Self-managing climate questionnaire

This questionnaire helps to identify the conditions in your organization in terms of various aspects or dimensions of the learning climate. Locate your organization or department on each of the following ten dimensions, ringing a number, from 1 to 7, to represent how you experience the climate in this respect. Try to avoid the middle ground.

1. *Physical environment* The amount and quality of space and privacy afforded to people; the temperature, ventilation, noise and comfort levels.

People are cramped for space, with little privacy and poor surroundings.

1 2 3 4 5 6 7

People have plenty of privacy and good physical conditions for managing themselves.

2. *Learning resources* The numbers, quality and availability of books, films, training packages, equipment, training staff and other resources for learning.

Very few or no resources; out-of-date and neglected equipment; only technical trainers.

1 2 3 4 5 6 7

Many resources - films, packages, books etc; up-to-date and well-maintained equipment; many training staff.

3. *Encouragement to learn* The extent to which people feel encouraged to try new things, take risks, experiment and learn new ways to do old tasks.

No encouragement to learn; no expectations to learn new skills and knowledge.

1 2 3 4 5 6 7

People are encouraged to try new ideas, to extend their skills and knowledge.

From Mike Pedler and Tom Boydell (1999) *Managing Yourself*, Lemos & Crane, London

4. How open and free are individuals in expressing feelings and opinions? Is there a free flow of information?

People never express feelings, secretive, and give few opinions. Information is hoarded and the flow impeded. 1 2 3 4 5 6 7 People are usually ready to are give their views and feelings, and readily pass on information.

5. *Rewards* The extent to which people feel they are rewarded for effort and recognized for good work rather than blamed or punished when things go wrong.

People are usually ignored but then blamed and criticized when things go wrong. 1 2 3 4 5 6 7 People are recognized for good work and rewarded for effort and creativity.

6. *Conformity to norms* The extent to which people are expected to conform to rules, regulations, policies and procedures rather than being given the responsibility to do their work as they think best.

People confirm to laid-down rules and standards at all times. Little personal responsibility is given or taken. 1 2 3 4 5 6 7 People do their work see as they fit; there is a great emphasis upon personal responsibility in the organization.

From Mike Pedler and Tom Boydell (1999) *Managing Yourself,* Lemos & Crane, London

7. *Value placed on ideas* How much are the ideas, opinions and suggestions of people sought out, encouraged and valued?

| People are 'not paid to think'; ideas are not valued. | 1 2 3 4 5 6 7 | Efforts are made to encourage people to put their ideas forward. There is a feeling that the future depends on people's ideas. |

8. **Practical help available** The extent to which people are ready to help each other by lending a hand, offering skills, knowledge or support.

| People don't help each unwillingness to pool or share resources. | 1 2 3 4 5 6 7 | People are very willing other; and helpful to each other; pleasure is taken in the success of others. |

9 *Warmth and support* The extent to which friendliness is considered important in the organization and the extent to which people support, trust and like one another.

| There is little warmth and support; this is a cold and isolating place to work. | 1 2 3 4 5 6 7 | This is a warm and friendly place;people enjoy coming to work. There is a belief that good relationships equals good work. |

From Mike Pedler and Tom Boydell (1999) *Managing Yourself*, Lemos & Crane, London

10. *Standards* The emphasis placed upon quality and standards and the extent to which members feel that challenging targets are set for themselves and for others.

Standards and quality are low; no one really cares very much.

1 2 3 4 5 6 7

Standards are high and challenging, people pick each other up and emphasize work quality.

SCORING
Add up your score. If it comes to 30 or less, then you're working in a poor climate as far as managing yourself (and probably many other things) is concerned. There's not a lot to encourage self-managing efforts here.

If you scored between 30 and 50 then your organization has an average climate in terms of encouraging the growth of initiative-taking and personal responsibility for managing better.

Above 50 and you have a favourable climate for self-managing. With this sort of support you should be able to survive trouble, maintain yourself in good condition, and develop your skills and abilities beyond their present level in order to deal with new tasks and problems.

From Mike Pedler and Tom Boydell (1999) *Managing Yourself*, Lemos & Crane, London

Activity 17: Structures and activities

Organizational resources, activities and structures which may offer openings for managing yourself

	I use this a lot	I don't use this much	I don't know about this
Resources and Materials • Books, bibliographies, reviews, databases • Journals, reports, paper • Newsletters, brochures • Packages • Films, videos, audio • Computers, intranet • Rooms, space, equipment • Other			
Activities and Processes • Training courses • Coaching, counselling • Job change, transfers, rotation, secondment • Visits • Appraisal interviews • Consultants, visitors • Conferences • Other			
Structures • Working parties, project teams • Teamwork meetings • Committees, e.g. health and safety, productivity, welfare, etc. • Quality circles • Workplace discussion groups • Trade unions, staff associations • 'Think tanks' • Professional associations • Luncheon clubs • Other			

From Mike Pedler and Tom Boydell (1999) *Managing Yourself*, Lemos & Crane, London

Index

NEW